A Fool's Errand

by

Steele MacKaye and Albion W. Tourgee

Edited, with an introduction by

Dean H. Keller

The Scarecrow Press, Inc.
Metuchen, N.J.   1969

To

The Memory Of

Sarah, Altie and Alice Phillips

Table of Contents

Introduction

In early February of the year 1881, while in
New York on a lecture tour, Albion W. Tourgée en-
countered Steele MacKaye at the Union League Club.[1]
In the course of their conversation they discussed the
possibility of collaborating on a dramatization of
Tourgée's popular novel of Reconstruction, A Fool's
Errand (1879). Tourgée's novel had been compared to
Uncle Tom's Cabin, and Tourgée was perhaps prompted
to seek this collaboration because of the success of the
dramatization of Mrs. Stowe's famous work and also
because of the rumored success of an unauthorized
dramatization of his novel.[2] MacKaye had already had
experience and success with adaptations and no doubt
was anxious to capitalize on the popularity of A Fool's
Errand.[3]

Before further discussions between the two busy
men could take place, Tourgée was called out of the
city. However, the two entered into a correspondence
which resulted in an agreement to write and produce
the play in the fall season of 1881.[4] The remainder
of the winter and spring was devoted to working out
the terms of the agreement under which the dramatization would be done. Finally, on May 20, Tourgée

wrote to MacKaye and submitted an eight point agreement or contract for his approval:

1.--S. M.--and A. W. T. -- agree to write together and own conjointly a play to be entitled "A Fool's Errand &c" to be founded on the novel of the same name written by the said A. W. T.--

2.--That the same shall be copyrighted as the said parties shall agree. The said A. W. T. as author of said novel assenting thereto as an adaptation thereof.

3.--That in case of any differences arising out of this collaboration, the same shall be settled by reference to arbitrators to be chosen one by either party and the two thus chosen shall have power to choose an umpire. in case of disagreement.

4.--That either party may notify the other to select an arbitrator and the name of the one he has chosen and if said party failed to do so in twenty-four hours after such notice, the arbitrator selected by the other shall decide. But in case any arbitrator cannot or will not act, the party selecting him shall propose another within one day and so on until one is secured.

5.--Said arbitrator shall decide within three days after being informed of the disagreement and to grounds, or have no further jurisdiction.

6.--The proceeds of said play shall be equally divided between the parties.

7.--The said parties shall agree upon a [word illegible] of [word illegible] and terms and a specific method for disposing, so as to protect and subserve the rights and interests of both, of said play to manager or presenting the same and in case of disagreement in regard thereto shall refer the same to arbitrators as before provided.

8.--Both of said parties shall give such time and labor as shall be necessary to complete said play by the ____day of____, 1881. [5]

Evidently MacKaye agreed to the terms of the contract outlined by Tourgée, for he responded, "If we are to do anything for next season we should get at the work at once...."[6]

The general business terms having been agreed upon, the collaborators set about the task of transforming Tourgée's didactic novel into a successful stage production. Tourgée was in the midst of a lecture tour, but he cancelled all engagements after June 28 and resolved to devote the rest of the summer to the dramatization.[7] MacKaye was busy winding up matters connected with his preceding season and in the process of planning for the next. Tourgée proposed to have a plot outline ready by June 22, and then, after MacKaye had time to study it, he suggested that the two meet to discuss details. The plan seemed logical and workable, but neither man could foresee the difficulties that were to follow. MacKaye was occupied with his other writing as well as with the innumerable details involved in managing an acting company, and he was constantly, so it seems, in financial difficulties. Tourgée, too, was involved in other writing, he was moving into a new home in western New York, and he and his family were troubled with ill health during much of the summer.

By July 5 it seems that no plot outline had been made, although the collaborators met in late June for consultation. [8] Tourgée wrote,

> I send you enclosed list of principal characters. You can infer from it the plan I am working on better than I could write it. I have concluded to adhere to Fool's Errand wherever possible and only add a few new characters. The scenes I have not yet fully decided upon. [9]

Work on the play proceeded slowly through July and August, although little progress is reported in the correspondence of July. Tourgée warned that three characters, Gaskill, 'Zouri, and Arthur Hyman, would require first rate talent, [10] although none of these characters appear in the final version of the play, at least not with these names. Two promotional ideas were forwarded by Tourgée at this time. MacKaye was encouraged to grant an interview to H. W. B. Howard of Fords, Howard, & Hulbert, Tourgée's publisher. Howard would in turn "... convert [the interview] into unpaid advertising notices for the [New York] Herald to your profit, mine, and incidently, of course, his own." [11] He also suggested that MacKaye could create a favorable climate for the première of their play in Philadelphia by saying that Tourgée, "... having lived there last winter,... met with so much kindness at the hands of the people that [he] insisted that they have the first opportunity to approve or con-

10

demn our work."[12]

The correspondence of August reveals a serious crisis in the financial affairs of Steele MacKaye, and there seemed to be some question as to whether or not A Fool's Errand could be produced at all. On July 29 Tourgée was confident he could provide $2,000 for the production, but on August 6, after a rather detailed recital of his own financial situation, he concluded: "I am sorry I consented to undertake this at all, but did not see how I could avoid it situated as you were."[13] Although several different sums of money were discussed, it can only be determined for certain that Tourgée contributed $850 to the project.[14]

On August 16, 1881, Tourgée mentioned, for the first time, that part of the play was actually written: "I send Ms--herewith of 1st act and more in day or two--"[15] The pace quickened in September and necessarily so, for the play was scheduled for production in October. On September 6 Tourgée sent MacKaye the fourth act and part of the third act with a promise to send the remainder of the third the next day. He also said he was at work on act five.[16] The arrangement seemed to be for the collaborators to pass the manuscripts back and forth, each making comments and suggestions. These were then incorporated into a new draft or version and passed around again.[17]

It seems that "...MacKaye's authority was to be supreme in matters of structure and Tourgée's in

11

matters of fact, but the two proved difficult to separate, and the author's didactics were inclined to
clash with the playwright's dramatic sense."[18] This
situation is strikingly illustrated in the collaborator's
correspondence. On September 11 Tourgée wrote to
MacKaye: "I send you herewith material which defines
the position of Southern young men upon the Ku Klux
question. It <u>must</u> come in somewhere as its elements
are <u>indispensible</u> to the success of the play."[19] This
is supposedly a matter of fact upon which Tourgée
was to be the supreme authority, but MacKaye later
confided: "Since I have cut out the political verbiage
of Judge Tourgée, and brought it down to my own
dramatic action, I have obtained laughter--applause--
silence--tears, precisely where I calculated upon doing so...."[20] In the same letter of September 11
Tourgée can be seen commenting upon what might be
called the structure of the play. Evidently MacKaye
had removed the death scene of Old Jerry Hunt and
Tourgée felt it should be reinstated. He reiterated
this feeling,[21] but MacKaye prevailed on this point
and Old Jerry was allowed to live.

And so the dramatization of <u>A Fool's Errand</u>
progressed with exchanges throughout late September
and early October. By October 10 the plan of the
play had been trimmed to four acts, but the fourth
act had yet to be written. Tourgée wrote, "I will go
at it and write a fourth act just as soon as I see how
you have left the 3d and can once see them all to-

gether and get their relations."[22]

The days before the first performance of the play were hectic. MacKaye's company was performing in various New York cities in late September, rehearsing the first part of A Fool's Errand between performances of Won at Last.[23] In mid-October he finished his tour and came to Philadelphia to make final arrangements for performances there. Act four of A Fool's Errand was not yet completed. MacKaye graphically described these circumstances in a letter to his wife two days after the opening at the Arch Street Theatre on October 26, 1881.

> My Dear Wife--I have not written because until now I have not had one moment. I have rehearsed from 9 in the morning until nearly 3 at night--stopping only for meals. Morris, my business manager, proved a total failure, so--while I was rehearsing the first three acts of the new play and acting at night--I had to attend to the business department also. Last week I had 9 performances besides the rehearsals. At the last moment, my leading actor ran away in a most cowardly manner. Meantime the fourth act was not yet written-- last Sunday was the only chance I got at it.

> I began in the morning, at Brooklyn--came on to Philadelphia in the afternoon--and, after doing a great deal of business connected with the play's management in the front of the house, I sat down at midnight and by five o'clock the next morning finished the play. I then routed O'Brien out of bed, got him to put it through the typewriter--and went to work myself condensing the other three acts. I did not take off my clothes at all--but was at rehearsal at nine in the morning--and re-

13

hearsal all day and night--having postponed
our first performance until Wednesday night.

Monday morning, when I arrived at the theatre for rehearsal, I received a telegram from
Graham curtly refusing at the last moment to
play Bill Sanders.--Here I was--with the 4th
act entirely unrehearsed--and two of the most
important parts not cast. You can imagine
how I felt. However there was nothing to do
but win, with the energy of the Devil himself.
I filled the two parts, and crowded into 3
days the work of 3 weeks. Our first performance would have done credit to any theatre in New York, and was received with great
enthusiasm by the audience. Yesterday I was
busy all day with cutting and rehearsing the
play again. I must now rush away to con-
tinue this work.... Yours J.S.M.[24]

The production attracted a good deal of attention.
It had strong performances by MacKaye as John Burleson and by F.F. Mackay as Uncle Jerry, and most of
the reviews were favorable.[25] The Philadelphia North
American of October 27 reported:

In concentrating Judge Tourgée's long novel
into a few, strong situations, Mr. MacKaye
has not tampered with his model as to destroy its identity; and it is gratifying, for
once, to see on the stage Southern people,
who are possessed of about the same faults
and virtues as the rest of the world and no
more, and to witness at the same time the
usual Northern contrast, without the accompaniment of suspenders and catarrh.... In the
dialogue there is a great deal of humour, and
much that is earnest,...yet before the close,
there is an appalling sense of surfeit. This
doubtless will find remedy, by cutting out a
large portion of the Ku Klux and 'nigger'
business.[26]

14

Although the critics praised the play and MacKaye reported that "The play is a genuine success--judged by its effect on the audience," he admitted that "The money success is, of course, very moderate."[27] A short time later MacKaye was asked in an interview if he was satisfied with the reception of A Fool's Errand. He replied:

> Perfectly. It has succeeded admirably in its intention, which was the illustration of a theme showing a political condition and its effect upon the people. As such, and as an entertaining picture of Southern and Northern character it is a great success.[28]

MacKaye closed his season in Philadelphia and began a disastrous tour, visiting St. Louis, Louisville, and Chicago, eventually returning to New York exhausted mentally and physically. He made an effort to revise A Fool's Errand while on the tour,[29] but it does not seem to have been successful and he did not revive the play.

The version of A Fool's Errand that has survived in the Albion W. Tourgée Papers is the four act version, probably close to the state in which it was performed on October 26. The broad outlines of Tourgée's narrative are present, but only vestiges of his message remain. To the cast of characters, Tourgée added four of importance: Maude Bradley, Bill Sanders, Achsah,[30] and Dennis McCarthy. The minor characters, Sam Irwin, Jim Smith, Sally and Winny, were given names, although their unnamed counterparts were in the novel.

Several of the scenes in the play have very definite origins in specific chapters of the novel. Act I is drawn from chapters nine and ten, Act III, scene 1, from chapter thirty-six, and Act III, scene 3, from chapter thirty-one. [31] The most sensational scene in the novel and play is the desperate ride by Lily Servosse to save her father from the Ku Klux Klan. The beginning of the scene provided an exciting curtain for Act II and its central portion carries over into scene 1 of Act III. MacKaye and Tourgée evidently counted on it to create a great theatrical effect. It is interesting to note that at least three editors included this scene from the novel in anthologies. [32]

When the play version of A Fool's Errand and the novel are compared, four significant differences seem to stand out. We are first confronted, at the opening of Act I, with the comic antics of Dennis McCarthy and Achsah, neither of whom appear in the novel. These additions, perhaps deemed necessary to relieve the serious aspects of the play, allowed a liberal use of both Irish and Negro accents, several songs, and some dances. More important was the death of Uncle Jerry Hunt, a problem for the playwrights already mentioned. Tourgée had written a very stark and powerful account of his hanging in the novel, [33] but in the play Uncle Jerry suffers an epileptic fit but does not die. The role of John Burleson has been greatly increased in the dramatization, even overshadowing Comfort Servosse, the hero of the novel.

16

Since Steele MacKaye himself played the part of Burleson, we can assume that he considered the part central. Finally, the resolution of the play is a positive one, with the two couples of young lovers united and Servosse and Burleson predicting a bright future for the south. The novel leaves us with no such feeling. Servosse dies and the future is looked upon as doubtful at best.

Albion W. Tourgée died in 1905 while in Bordeaux, France, serving as United States Consul. On her return to the United States, Tourgée's wife Emma was contacted by John Brisben Walker about the possibility of dramatizing A Fool's Errand.[34] Evidently he did not know of the earlier work by MacKaye and Tourgée, but Mrs. Tourgée informed him of it and offered to send him the manuscript. Walker agreed to read it but he warned that he did". . . not feel much confidence in anything MacKaye has done."[35] This fleeting interest in a dramatic version of A Fool's Errand was very likely prompted by the controversy created by the novels and plays of Thomas Dixon. Nothing came of Walker's idea, and since 1906 there has, of course, been no interest in a revival of this play and very little awareness of its existence.

The text of A Fool's Errand published here is from the only manuscript known to exist. This version was copyrighted by Tourgée and MacKaye, in accordance with their contract, on August 12, 1881 (Copyright # 12511). It was never published and all

17

acting copies seem to have disappeared. The play is typewritten on the recto of forty leaves measuring eight inches by 12 inches. Only the text reproduced on pages 28 through 107 is from the manuscript. The lists of characters and scenes were provided by the editor.

This copy of A Fool's Errand is a part of the Albion W. Tourgée Papers in the Chautauqua County Historical Society at Westfield, New York. The editor wishes to acknowledge the assistance of the Society, especially Mr. Roderick A. Nixon, and to thank the Society for permission to quote from the play and from material in that collection which is cited in this Introduction. He also wishes to thank the Society for allowing him the use of their unique manuscripts. He is also greatly indebted to the Dartmouth College Libraries for permitting the use of important papers from the Steele MacKaye Collection.

The editor wishes to acknowledge, with gratitude, the encouragement and assistance of Professors Paul T. Nolan and James M. Salem in bringing this work to a successful conclusion.

Kent State University Libraries
Kent, Ohio

Notes for the Introduction

1. Percy MacKaye, Epoch; The Life of Steele Mac-
Kaye, Genius of the Theatre, In Relation to His Times
& Contemporaries (New York: Boni & Liveright, 1927),
Vol. I, p. 416.

2. Otto H. Olsen, Carpetbagger's Crusade: The Life
of Albion W. Tourgée (Baltimore: Johns Hopkins University Press, 1965), p. 253.   In the Albion W.
Tourgée Papers in the Chautauqua County Historical
Society at Westfield, New York [hereafter cited as
Tourgée Papers] are four posters advertising a production of A Fool's Errand by Field's Combination,
managed by Alf. Newton Field.   Three of the posters
were printed by the Blade Printing and Paper Company
of Toledo, Ohio, and the other, a lithograph, was
made in Cleveland by W. J. Morgan and Company.
No dates or places of performance appear on the
posters.   Tourgée's name is mentioned in the ad-
vertisement but he is not actually connected with the
dramatization of the novel.   The following paragraph
appears on one of the posters:

> The American Public having for years witnessed
> the Anti-Bellum Play of Uncle Tom's Cabin,
> are, to use the words of a celebrated journalist,

'panting for something as interesting and edifying.' The dramatists' brain has been puzzled to fill that want, and at last Judge Tourgée has given a book to the world which gives the theme. The play was advertised as "The Greatest Sensation of the Age" and it contained such scenes as "The Ride for Life," "The Ku Klux Klan in Council" and "The Hanging of Old Uncle Jerry." From these few facts--MacKaye is not mentioned, Tourgée is not actually connected with the dramatization, and Uncle Jerry does not die in the version of the play which is considered here-- we may infer that the posters refer to the unauthorized production which concerned Tourgée in 1881.

3.   MacKaye, op. cit., Vol. II, p. xvi.   MacKaye had adapted plays by Octave Feuillet, Ernest Blum, and Victor Hugo.

4.   Tourgée to MacKaye, 7 May 1881.   Steele Mac-Kaye Papers, Dartmouth College, Hanover, New Hampshire [hereafter cited as MacKaye Papers].

5.   Tourgée to MacKaye, 20 May 1881.   MacKaye Papers.

6.   MacKaye to Tourgée, 8 June 1881.   Tourgée Papers.

7.   Tourgée to MacKaye, 10 June 1881 and 14 June 1881.   MacKaye Papers.

8. Tourgée to MacKaye, 5 July 1881. MacKaye Papers.

9. Ibid.

10. Ibid.

11. Tourgée to MacKaye, 25 July 1881. MacKaye Papers.

12. Tourgée to MacKaye, 29 July 1881. MacKaye Papers.

13. Tourgée to MacKaye, 6 August 1881. MacKaye Papers.

14. Cancelled checks from Tourgée to MacKaye as follows: 23 September 1881, $300; 30 September 1881, $300; 7 October 1881, $250. Tourgée Papers.

15. Tourgée to MacKaye, 16 August 1881. MacKaye Papers.

16. Tourgée to MacKaye, 6 September 1881. Mac-Kaye Papers. The play was eventually completed in four acts.

17. Tourgée to MacKaye, 11 September 1881, 22 September 1881, MacKaye Papers, and MacKaye,

op. cit. , Vol. I, p. 418, 25 September 1881.

18. Olsen, op. cit. , pp. 253-4.

19. Tourgée to MacKaye, 11 September 1881. Mac-
Kaye, op. cit. , Vol. I, p. 417.

20. MacKaye to Mrs. MacKaye, 29 October 1881.
Ibid. , p. 425.

21. Tourgée to MacKaye, 22 September 1881. MacKaye
Papers.

22. Tourgée to MacKaye, 10 October 1881. MacKaye
Papers.

23. MacKaye, op. cit. , Vol. I, p. 419.

24. MacKaye to Mrs. MacKaye, 26 October 1881.
Ibid. , pp. 421-2.

25. Ibid. , p. 424.

26. Quoted in Ibid. , p. 423.

27. MacKaye to Mrs. MacKaye, 29 October 1881.
Ibid. , p. 425.

28. Interview with Steele MacKaye, New York Dra-

matic Mirror, January 14, 1882, p. 7.

29. MacKaye to Mrs. MacKaye, 2, 3, 4 November 1881. MacKaye, op. cit., Vol. I, p. 425.

30. Probably a renaming of the 'Zouri mentioned in the letter from Tourgée to MacKaye, 5 July 1881, MacKaye Papers. 'Zouri is a character in Tourgée's book A Royal Gentleman and 'Zouri's Christmas (New York: Fords, Howard and Hulbert, 1881).

31. Albion W. Tourgée, A Fool's Errand (New York: Fords, Howard and Hulbert, 1879).

32. Dean H. Keller, "A Checklist of the Writings of Albion W. Tourgée (1838-1905)," Studies in Bibliography, XVIII (1965), 273-274.

33. Tourgée, op. cit., pp. 201-208.

34. John Brisben Walker to Emma Tourgée, 24 March 1906. Tourgée Papers.

35. John Brisben Walker to Emma Tourgée, 30 March 1906. Tourgée Papers.

A FOOL'S ERRAND

Dramatis Personae

Comfort Servosse

Mrs. Servosse, his wife

Lily, their daughter

Maude Bradley, a school teacher

John Burleson, a Southern gentleman

Melville Gurney, a Southern gentleman

Jayheu Brown, a Southern Unionist

Uncle Jerry Hunt, a Negro leader

Achsah, his daughter

Dennis McCarthy, a servant of Servosse

Bill Sanders

Sam Irwin   members of the Ku Klux Klan

Jim Smith

Sally   Negroes

Winny

Soldiers

Negroes

Ku Klux Klansmen

Scenes
Act I: The Garden at Warrington
Act II: The Sitting Room at Warrington

27

Act III:
    Scene 1:   Black Rock Glen
    Scene 2:   Exterior of Jayheu Brown's House
    Scene 3:   Exterior of Uncle Jerry Hunt's Cabin
Act IV: The Sitting Room at Warrington

Time: Shortly After the Civil War
Place: North Carolina

ACT I

Scene. A garden among the trees at Warrington.
Rustic seats R. & L.; flag-staff C.

At rise enter DENNIS, with American flag;
singing "Rally Round the Flag,"; xes C. to pole.

ACHSAH [off r.]. Hi--Ya-Ya--Ya-Ya!
DENNIS [starts]. Who's there--is that you Achsah?
Why don't ye answer me ye nagur witch?
MRS. SERVOSSE [enters porch L.]. Dennis, have you
seen Achsah this morning?
DENNIS. Divil a bit--axin' yer pardin ma'am--an' may
I nivir see the haythin nagur agin ma'am!
MRS. S. Why what have you against the girl?
DENNIS. Everything ma'am--First, she's a witch!
MRS. S. [laughing]. Achsah a witch?
DENNIS. Yis--A witch she is an' nothin' else.
Sphake low--Sure there's no knowin' what lafe their
hid under--She an' that white-wooled ould quadruped,
her father!
MRS. S. Dennis you must not speak ill of Uncle
Jerry. He is a good ole man, though sadly af-
flicted, and has been of great service to us since
we came here!

29

DENNIS. Oh, the divil take the day we came to this
place ma'am. I think yer husband the Karnel--jist
run on a fool's errand, when he came here among
these nagurs and ribels, wid everything wrong from
what it ought to be. Look at the day now--Here's
June weather for Thanksgivin'!

MRS. S. So much the better--We can enjoy it out-
doors as well as within, and so have invited our
neighbors to celebrate it with us. [xes L.]

DENNIS. Aye--But ye've asked the nagurs too!

MRS. S. Of course--They have most cause to give
thanks!

DENNIS. Bedad if I were black, I'd not give thanks
for anythin', till the mark o' Cain was off me hide.

MRS. S. But if you'd been a slave all your life, and
suddenly you were set free.

DENNIS. Och--I'd be thankful enough thin. Sure even
a cur thanks God with his tail when his collar's
off!

MRS. S. Well then hoist that flag Dennis, and let us
thank God it still floats over the whole land!

DENNIS. Be me sowl we will ma'am!

MRS. S. [on steps]. There--I think everything is
ready for the Thanksgiving table. As soon as the
flag is raised Dennis, come into the house. [ext.]

DENNIS. I will ma'am! [sings "Rally Round," hoist-
ing flag up.]

ACHSAH. [off r.]. Hi Ya-Ya! Scatch! Scatch!

DENNIS. [starts]. Whisht--That nise again--Achsah

30

I say--Is that you? [ACHSAH steals in behind him]
Can't ye answer a civil question ye haythin brat?
[ACHSAH cuts off a lock of his hair; jumps C. with
wild yell. DENNIS turns in terror] Hi--Howly
Moses--It's Achsah. What are ye at ye wild nagur?
[ACHSAH holds up hair; brandishes scissors] Be-
gorra--Cuttin' off a lock of me hair widout lave.
Ye thafe of the world--What dy'e mane? [starts to-
ward her]
ACHSAH [stops him with gesture]. Jes stop whar yo'
is--I'll sho' yo'! [blows on hair; waves it about;
dances]

> Blow, blow, south wind hot!
> Blow, blow--east wind dry!
> Fade and wrinkle--dry and rot!
> Shrivel arm and wither eye!

DENNIS [aside]. Och sure she's invokin' the powers
of darkness on me! Oh, Axy darlin'--Would ye
charm a poor boy's life away, in broad daylight--
Sure ye'll get into trouble dear!
ACHSAH. Yo won't make much trouble, if I jes blow
dis yer ha'r to Obi!
DENNIS. Saints defind us, an' who's Mr. Obi?
ACHSAH. Dat's nigger for debbil!
DENNIS. The divil it is!
ACHSAH. Yes--an' he's my fren'!
DENNIS. Och Alanna--Axy darlin'--Axy--What--What'll
ye take for the hair?
ACHSAH. Niffin! While I'se got dis, yo's got to do

jes what I tells yo' an' can't hep yo'sef nuther!

DENNIS. Oh powers above dy'e hear that? [xes l.]

ACHSAH [xes r.]. Yo' know my Daddy?

DENNIS. The ould gintlemin wid de white hair, that wears a pair o' canes?

ACHSAH. Dat's him. Will yo' be good to dat ole man, an' hep' him ef he's in trouble?

DENNIS. The divil take me if I don't!

ACHSAH. Dat's all right. Jes' take car yo' do dat, or I'll blow dis yer ha'r to Obi shore--an' ef I do dat, yo'll jes' hab de debbil's luck fo' de rest ob yo' life--So take ca'r massa Dennis, take ca'r-- I'se gwine now--but I'se got yo' ha'r--an'--well jes look out fo' Obi's roun--Obi! Obi! [exit r.2]

DENNIS [shudders]. Sure I'm shiverin' in the sunshine. Och alanna, why was I born to see this day. She's got me hair an' I'm witched! [starts; catches elbow] Och, murther--There it is--in me elbow-- the sting o' the divil. Och, mercy, in me legs too! [dances about] Och--Hould on Axy--Be Axy me darlin'--Have marcy--I'll do anythin ye say--I will-- I will--Och! Och! Och!

BURLESON [enters r.3; slaps whip on seat]. Hello!

DENNIS [turns with howl]. Mr. Burleson--as I'm a sinner!

BURL. What's the row Dennis?

DENNIS. Lord sor--I'm witched--by that black baste Axy!

BURL. At her old tricks again--eh? [laughs]

32

DENNIS. Sure sor--you wouldn't laugh if you were witched!

BURL. Dennis--I am bewitched!

DENNIS. Lord love ye sor--Has Achsah been at you too?

BURL. Oh Achsah be hanged!

DENNIS. Amin sor--Amin--But who's witched you sor?

BURL. A woman!

DENNIS. Av coorse--What else could it be?

BURL. The last one in the world that ought to be able to do it too!

DENNIS. That's always the way wid 'em!

MRS. S. [off l.]. Dennis--Oh Dennis!

DENNIS. Aye, aye, ma'am!

MRS. S. Oh, Dennis--You're wanted!

DENNIS. Yis ma'am--an' I'm comin'!

BURL. Dennis! [D. turns] Is--is Miss Bradley in?

DENNIS. Is it the nagur schoolma'am ye mane sor?

BURL. Damn the schoolma'am! No, no--I don't mean that--Is she in?

DENNIS. No sir--not yet! [laughs]

BURL. What are you laughing at?

DENNIS. Oh, nothin' sir--nothin' [laughs] Bedad--she's caught him sure enough! She's got a lock of his hair! [exit porch]

BURL. I believe that idiot suspects my secret; I wonder if she does. Just think of it--I, John Burleson--A southern gentleman. She, a nigger schoolteacher --And I come sneaking around here. No--I won't be

33

such an ass--I'll go! [starts r.]

MAUDE. [laughs off r.].

BURL. [stops; drops whip]. Her voice--Her laugh!
[picks up whip; sits] I give in--No use--Hanged if
I can go now!

MAUDE. [enters; with two little mulattoes; her arms
full of bundles; xes table l.; distributing them].
Here-Sally--you take these--and you, Winny, these--
now be off! [pats their heads; they exit l.]

BURL. Damnation! [she turns in surprise] I beg
pardon--I---

MAUDE. Mr. Burleson! You? Here?

BURL. Yes, I believe I am--and I say Maud---Miss
Bradley I mean--aren't you ashamed of yourself?

MAUDE. Ashamed--of what?

BURL. Petting niggers!

MAUDE. Oh, is that all? I have seen you petting
your horse and your dog too.

BURL. Of course you have!

MAUDE [laughs]. Now sir--Are not you ashamed?
Are not these little colored girls as good as dogs
sir?

BURL. Well suppose they are?

MAUDE. Well then--you'd better drop the subject!

BURL. What's the matter with you anyhow? You're
as kind as a kitten to those niggers--Can't you be
a bit civil to a white man. Blessed if I don't believe you think a nigger better than a white man--
anyway!

34

MAUDE. That sir depends upon who the white man is!

BURL. That's meant for me I reckon!

MAUDE. If it fits you--yes!

BURL. [starts off]. Thank you--Good day, Miss Bradley!

MAUDE. [pretending to let a bundle fall on hand]. Oh dear!

BURL. [returning]. By Jove--Are you hurt?

MAUDE. A little!

BURL. I'm infernally sorry!

MAUDE [archly]. Honest!

BURL. Yes--with all my heart!

MAUDE. All your heart! [laughs] I don't believe you've got any!

BURL. That's true--I haven't now--I had once--I don't believe you ever had one.

MAUDE. Don't you really?

BURL. Do I don't!

MAUDE [archly]. Honest?

BURL. Honest. I wish you had a heart!

MAUDE. Why?

BURL. That I might try to win it!

MAUDE [laughs]. You--John Burleson, try to win the heart of a Yankee schoolma'am?

BURL. Oh--the dev--Don't remind me of that now!

MAUDE. And why not sir--I'd rather be a Yankee schoolma'am, than a southern rebel any day!

BURL. I'm a southern gentleman Miss Bradley!

MAUDE. Oh, yes--and so think work a disgrace!

BURL. No, not now--I did once perhaps--before the war. When that was over, I had nothing but a bare plantation left. Then I thought of my mother and sisters, and didn't stop to ask questions. I just kicked off my old confed uniform--hitched my horse to a bull-tongue--hired some niggers--went to work. There wasn't a better crop in the whole south this year than mine!

MAUDE. No? You're more a man than I thought! [hand out] Shake!

BURL. [grasps it]. If you'd only give up those infernal niggers!

MAUDE [snatches hand away]. Give them up--Why?

BURL. Because southern society will never receive a nigger teacher!

MAUDE [laughs]. I didn't come here to seek a reception from society. I left a happy home full of friends to do what I could for the ignorant and helpless creatures whom God had set free. I'm not ashamed of my work sir, and I don't care to call anyone friend who is. Do you understand?

BURL. I do!

MAUDE. Honest?

BURL. Yes--Honest!

MAUDE. Well what have you to say to it?

BURL. Nothing to you--A man can't argue with a woman. If you were only a man.

MAUDE. Well?

BURL. No matter--I'm going!

36

MAUDE. You said that before.

BURL. I mean it now! [going]

MAUDE [looks r.; angrily]. I declare--There he is again!

BURL [returns]. Who?

MAUDE [affected surprise]. I thought you'd gone!

BURL. I am gone--Dead gone!

MAUDE. Oh, nonsense--Look there!

BURL. What is it?

MAUDE. Melville Gurney riding with Lily Servosse!

BURL. Well--what of it?

MAUDE. Lily is my dearest friend sir--and it makes by blood boil to see that!

BURL. What do you mean!

MAUDE. Mr. Gurney prides himself on being a southern gentleman--but no gentleman would ever trifle with the love of a trusting girl!

BURL [fires up]. I don't understand you Miss Bradley--but Melville Gurney is my friend, and as gallant a man as ever rode a horse or drew a sword.

MAUDE. Yet he seeks to win her love by stealth!

BURL. I tell you Gurney is incapable of anything dishonorable.

MAUDE. Then why doesn't he act like a man and come openly to her father's house.

BURL. How should I know? I mind my own business, and let other people take care of theirs! [xes.]

MAUDE. And my business sir is to think of my friend's welfare. Woe to the man who dares to trifle with her--I'd horsewhip him with my own hands.

BURL [whistles]. What a grand little woman she is--
if she does teach niggers.

MAUDE. Ah--They're here--He's helping her off. I
declare he's coming in with her!

GURNEY [off r.; laughs]. And are you still frightened?

LILY. Not much--But the place will haunt me as long
as I live! [enters with him] Oh, Maude--I'm so
glad you're here--Mr. Gurney--Maude! [they ex-
change bows coldly]

GURNEY. Hello John--You here. I haven't seen you
in a coon's age--Where have you been? [xes l. to
him]

BURL. At work old boy!

LILY. What do you confess to such a thing as work--
I can't believe it!

BURL. Look at my hands--They speak for me! [holds
them out]

LILY [looks at them]. Let me shake them Mr. Burleson. Hard hands go best with warm and honest
hearts!

MAUDE. What kept you so long dear?

LILY [seated l. with M.] I met Mr. Gurney and he
took me to a wonderful place, called Black Rock
Glen!

BURL [aside l.]. The devil!

MAUDE. What a cheerful name!

LILY. Oh the place is worse than its name. It terri-

38

fied me--It was so dark and grim!

MAUDE. A strange place for a gentleman to take a lady sir!

GURNEY. Well yes perhaps so--But I meant no harm!

MAUDE. It is well you did not sir!

GURNEY [to BURL]. What in the deuce does she mean? [both l.]

BURL. Gurney--you're a fool. Don't you know that glen is one of the meeting places of our Klan?

GURNEY. The Ku Klux--By Jove I entirely forgot it!

BURL. You may have reason to remember it!

GURNEY. Did you receive my note?

BURL. Yes--Take care to be prompt at the council of Den No. 9. Walters may be doomed by the Klan unless we're there to oppose the dangerous men who have crept into our ranks!

GURNEY. You can count on me to back you in saving Walter's life!

LILY. Mr. Gurney--Let us walk into the house. Won't you join us Mr. Burleson?

BURL. Thanks--Later perhaps--I have some business to attend to first!

LILY. Oh, very well Mr. Burleson. Come Mr. Gurney--Come Maude!

MAUDE [picks up bundles]. I'll be with you in a moment! [LILY and GURNEY exit l.]

BURL. May I help you Miss Bradley?

MAUDE. Thanks--I can help myself.

BURL. You are cruel!

MAUDE. Do you really think so?

BURL. I do indeed!

MAUDE. Honest?

BURL. Yes honest!

MAUDE [laughs]. So much the better! Good bye!
[exit l.]

BURL. [looks after]. God bless her! And yet what
a madman I am. What would my mother and sisters say, if they knew I loved that little woman. A
precious row there'd be!

BILL SANDERS [off r.]. Get out of the way you
black thieves!

SAM IRWIN [off r.]. Don't get in a white man's path
--Clar the road niggers!

ACHSAH [off r.]. Here dar--Yo' jes stop--Don't yo'
go to hitten' my ole dad--or I'll kill yo'--Yo' mean
low down white trash!

BURL. [looks r.]. That crazy creature Achsah in
trouble again--And Uncle Jerry--her father too!

VOICES [off r.]. That's right--Stir 'em up--Go for
'em--Ha, Ha, Ha!

ACHSAH [entering; defending UNCLE JERRY. BILL,
SAM and JIM follow; teasing her]. Jes' leab us
alone. We ain't a doin' nuffin' to yo'. Stan' back
dar, or I'll jes tear yo' eyes out--I will! [trash
recoil down l.] Oh, Massa Burleson, won't yo' keep
dese low-down white trash offen us?

BURL. What are you doing here gal? [r.]

JERRY [c.; removes hat]. Sarven' Massa Burleson!

40

Dis be Thanksgibben' day, an' Kernel S'vosse tole
us t come up hea', an' hab a good time a-tankin'
de Lo'd fo' all his bressins!

BURL. Well--what have these men been doing to you?

BILL. We hain't done nuthin' to 'em. We was comin'
up here to see the fun, an' them two got in our
road--The derned no-account niggers!

ACHSAH. We hain't no niggers nuther--We's jes' as
good as yo. We's free now an' got jes as much
right to de road as de white folks. Sech low-down
mean white trash as yo', ain't fit ter 'sociate wid
niggers!

JERRY. Sho, sho honey--Don't go on dat er way now!

BURL. If you wish to keep your people out of trouble,
teach them to keep their places and have civil
tongues in their heads.

JERRY. Sartin Massa sartin. Dats what I tries ter do.

BURL. You niggers are getting too infernally free.

JERRY. De Lo'd has made us free Massa!

BURL. You mean the Yanks have made you free to
work and take care for yourselves--but not to lie
around and loaf and brag as if you were the equals
of white folks!

TRASH. Good! Good!

BURL. Come, come--I don't want any of your approval! Look here Uncle, you've been tryin' to spoil
my niggers lately--enticing them off to school as
you call it. This won't do--Don't try it again--dy'e
hear?

41

JERRY. Massa Burleson, I hears--but all de same
I'se boun' ter do it. I means ter lead my peple
out ob de darkness fo' de glory ob de Lo'd!

BURL. Oh, hang your can't. If you don't leave my
niggers alone I'll make you!

JERRY. Yo' can't do dat. Nuffin ull eber stop ole
Jerry from a' doin' his dooty to his peple sah!
[raises cane solemnly] An' yo'd better take ca'r
Massa Burleson, an' not stan' in de way ob de Lo'd.
Mind yer--He's de Lo'd Almighty an' 'll grind yer
ter powdah ef yo' do!

BILL [to others]. Jes' listen to the damn nigger's
threats!

BURL. Uncle Jerry you know me?

JERRY. Eber sence yo' was a babby. Nussed and
toted yo' 'bout, menny a time, when I b'longed to
yo' Pa Massa Burleson!

BURL. You know I tell the truth then?

JERRY. Nebber know'd yo' ter tell a lie--dat's a fac!

BURL. Well let me tell you. The next time you coax
my niggers off the plantation, he'll lose his place
and have you to thank for it! [xing to trash] What
do you want here?

BILL. Come to see the Yankee blow-out!

BURL. You're not to raise any row here--Do you understand?

BILL. Nary row--Mr. Burleson!

BURL. And see that you leave these niggers alone--
dy'e hear? [xes.]

42

BILL. All right! But--Oh, Burleson!

BURL. [turns]. Well what do you want?

BILL [goes to him c.; looks around furtively]. I'm one of the Klan now you know!

BURL. You?

BILL. Yes--Here's the countersign! Camelia! There's to be a meeting at Den No. 10 to-night. Now don't you forget that I'm a brother Klucker!

BURL. [aside; going]. When creatures like this join the ranks, it's time gentlemen fell out! [has dropped note from pocket; exit. music]

BILL [picks up note]. Hello--What's this. By gad-- A letter from Gurney to Burleson about the Klan. Thet's lucky--This may be worth a good deal to me yit--I'll take durned good keer on it too!

ACHSAH [fixes toilet]. Dar now Daddy--I guess we'se ready to go in de kitchen--an' make 'em open dar eyes--Come 'long!

BILL [grasping ACHSAH'S arm]. Hold on you sassy nigger. Jim--you look after the ole man--Sam and I'll take keer o' the gal!

ACHSAH. Stan' back dar or I'll scream! [BILL and SAM struggle with her]

BILL [hand round neck]. There now Sam--Off with her toggery. We'll take the impudence out of her! [SERVOSSE enters r.; runs down; knocks BILL down. ACHSAH throws SAM off]

JERRY. De Kernel--Bress de Lo'd!

BILL [rising]. Who are you?

43

SERV. Master here--Leave!

BILL. By gad--No derned Yankee shall insult me!
Take that! [aims pistol]

SERV. [catches his arm; flings him down; wrenches
pistol from him. SAM springs for him. raises
pistol. SAM recoils l.] Take care! You may get
hurt!

SAM. Look out--They're coming from the house.
[exits quickly with JIM]

SERV. Now go! [puts pistol in pocket] Guess I'll
confiscate this!

BILL [going. shakes fist at him]. By gad--I'll get
even with you yit! [exit. All enter hastily]

MRS. S. Oh, Comfort--I'm so glad you're back!

LILY. We thought we heard a scream!

SERV. Oh, nothing dear but some of Achsah's nonsense!

LILY [embracing him]. Oh, I'm so glad it's nothing
more!

SERV. Ah, Mr. Gurney--I'm glad we have you here
to-day!

GURNEY. May I say one word to you aside sir?

SERV. Certainly! Be seated sir I am at your service!
[MAUDE and MRS. S. exeunt l. with JERRY & ACH-
SAH. LILY lingers back]

GURNEY. Colonel Servosse, I have come to tell you
that you do not understand the temper of our people,
and to warn you to beware of it.

SERV. I don't quite take your meaning!

GURNEY. Well sir I regret to say that a dangerous feeling is growing up in our community against you sir!

SERV. And why?

GURNEY. Because sir, the teachers of the colored schools are your guests; sit at your table, and to-day their pupils are to be entertained upon your plantation!

SERV. Undoubtedly!

GURNEY. Well sir--pardon me if I feel forced to tell you that southern society cannot recognize those who make nigger teachers their familiar associates.

SERV. Mr. Gurney, I know the teachers of the colored schools. They are ladies of character and culture engaged in a noble work. While I have a house it shall shelter them at their need or my pleasure. I think we understand each other now--Permit me to say good day!

GURNEY [going]. Good day sir!

LILY [c.] You've not been quarrelling with my father?

GURNEY. We disagree--I trust we may never quarrel!

LILY. And you won't stay now?

GURNEY. I wish I could.

LILY. Why can't you?

GURNEY. I--I will tell you to-morrow--Till then good bye! [extends hand]

LILY. [takes it]. Good bye! [looks after. he exits]

SERV. Lily!

LILY [coming down]. Well father?

45

SERV. Do you know why young Gurney won't stop to-
day?

LILY. No--I can't imagine!

SERV. Well it's because Maude Bradley is our guest!

LILY. What has he against her?

SERV. She's a nigger teacher!

LILY. Is that his reason for going away!

SERV. His one noble reason!

LILY. Then he may stay away forever!

SERV. [embracing her]. Spoken like my own true
child. Bless me--What's this? Tears!

LILY. Nothing--nothing! But to think of dear Maude
being so insulted! [sobs] Oh, I must go to her at
once! [exits l.]

SERV. [sits]. Well, well--I didn't look for this sort
of thing--Gurney's a good man too. Will the old
spirit never die?

JAYHEU BROWN [has entered; coming down]. Not ez
long as white's white, an black's black, an' they
both on 'em think t'other's green!

SERV. I don't understand you sir!

BROWN. Nuther do I--I never did--an' I never will--
Wal no--I reckon not, taint menny az does understand me; I don't think I quite understand myself!

SERV. Excuse me sir--but I believe I have not the
honor of your acquaintance.

BROWN. No--Thet's so sir--Jayheu Brown--Thet's my
name! [coughs]

SERV. Not Jayheu Brown, who piloted our boys

through the mountains after they'd escaped from
Salisbury?

BROWN. Yes! [coughs] I'm thet man!

SERV. A southern Union man--Bravest of the brave!
[shakes his hand warmly] I'm glad to see you sir--
and proud to welcome you to my house!

BROWN [coughs]. Thank ye sir--thank ye!

SERV. Be seated sir--You seem to have a bad cough,
Mr. Brown.

BROWN. I reckon it mought seem bad to a stranger
sir--but I've seen the day I wouldn't take no money
fer thet cough! [coughs] No amount!

SERV. So?

BROWN. Yis--That cough was my exemption paper
Colonel!

SERV. Your exemption paper--I don't understand!

BROWN. Wal yo' see every now and then--durin' the
war, some uv my neighbors ud git the notion thet
Jayheu Brown ought ter go and fight fer the Confed-
eracy! [coughs] So, they'd go an' see the conscript
officer. Then I'd go en see him, an' get sent afore
the examinin' board--an' I mus' say thar wasn't nary
board--no matter who was on it thet wouldn't say
t'was jest a waste uv transportation ter send me on
ter camp--atter they'd heard me cough--when it was
right holler! [coughs]

SERV. Gracious! I should think so--I wonder you're
alive!

BROWN. Thet's what the doctors said afore I buried

'em. They said 'twas a miracle I was alive--Tho'
I've managed to pull through some tollable close
places with thet exemption paper; it's done me a
power of good mister--a power of good! [coughs]

SERV. But you don't need it now?

BROWN. Not jest now--but thar's no knowin' how soon
it may come in handy agin!

SERV. Do you think a little sperits ud do it good?

BROWN. Well now you speak on it Colonel--I don't
mind ef I do take a small dram with you.

SERV. Will you have it here or step into the house?

BROWN. Right here squire--ef it's all the same to
you.

SERV. Certainly! Dennis--Oh, Dennis I say!

DENNIS [inside l.]. Aye, aye sor!

SERV. Bring us some whiskey!

DENNIS. All right sor!

BROWN [Negroes sing in distance]. Eh Colonel--
what's that?

SERV. The colored people singing on their way here
to celebrate Thanksgiving!

BROWN. Oh yis this is Thanksgiving day--I done forgot all about is--So the nigger's is coming here.
Colonel ef you don't mind a stranger sayin' on it, I
must tell ye, yer makin' too much of these darkies
fer yer own good!

DENNIS [has entered down c.]. Bedad that's so--Ye
niver said a truer word, whoever ye are!

SERV. Dennis when I want your opinion I'll ask for it.

48

DENNIS. Thank ye sor, an' I'll give it ye in the plainest brogue I can--an' for nothin'. [bus.] Here's the whiskey yer honor! [bus. of drinking]

SERV. How will you take it Mr. Brown?

BROWN. Clar an' straight Colonel; I don't never take it, unless I needs it, or has a hankerin' fer it! [coughs] An' then I counts it a dooty sir, [coughs] an' makes it a pleasure! My regards sir! [drinks]

DENNIS. [aside]. The ould party looks like a stall-fed ghost! Whiskey straight an' plenty ov it! Faith he's sinsible to the last! Whiskey straight! [smacks lips; exits]

BROWN. I've jes' come to let ye know, that the Ku Klux hev begun thar work in this county Colonel!

SERV. Is it possible?

BROWN. Yes sir! [coughs] They've begun with the darkies and I 'llow they'll not stop till they've got some uv us Unioners out uv the way! Judge Denton wanted I should tell you, thet Walter's life is in danger, an' he wants you to go into town at once, an' I reckon you'd better go Colonel.

SERV. I will. The moment these colored people arrive I'll slip away with you! [singing nearer] Ah--Here they are! [enter all from house]

LILY. Oh--They're coming--They're coming!

MRS. S. Yes--and see how happy the poor things look! [enter Negroes led by ACHSAH; singing]

CHORUS.   Free, free, my Lo'd free,
            An, we walks de hebbenly way,

49

ACHSAH.　　Ole satin's like a huntin houn'!
CHORUS.　　Free, my Lo'd free,
ACHSAH.　　Chase de sinner roun' an' roun'!
CHORUS.　　Free, my Lo'd free!
ACHSAH.　　Gabriel blow de little ho'n!
　　　　　　Sinner's free, and satin's boun'!
CHORUS.　　Free, my Lo'd free,
　　　　　　An' we walks de hebbenly way!
SERV. My friends you are welcome. Today a free
　　people makes Thanksgiving, throughout the whole
　　land. I have invited you and your teachers to join
　　in our festival, and in your joy to devoutly remem-
　　ber the great giver of all good things!
NEGROES. Amen--Bress de Lo'd! Free cheers fer
　　de Kernel! [cheers]
JERRY. Jes' one moment ef you please. Colonel
　　S'vosse, an' you ladies and gemmen--It's true we's
　　free. It was de Lo'd wuk--But you northern men
　　and women was his bressed instruments. We can't
　　tank him widout a-tankin' you--So yo'll be in our
　　prars ter day long side of dat bressed martyr Lin-
　　kum--- [all remove hats; kneel] Dat libs in our
　　hearts ebery day an' night an' can't neber be forgot!
NEGROES. [rising]. Amen--Dat's so--Go on Uncle
　　Jerry--Go on!
JERRY. Hush now chillun--An' listen to de Kunnel!
ACHSAH. Free cheers fer de Kernel! [cheers]
SERV. My friends I thank you for the kindly feelings
　　you entertain toward us, and can only assure you

50

that we shall remain your friends as long as you by hard work and good conduct prove yourselves worthy of friendship! [cheers. a horn off L.] But there-- the horn speaks for me and welcomes you to the kitchen, where you will find a Thanksgiving dinner awaiting your attack! Now go--and God bless you all!

JERRY [bowing; turning away]. Tank you Massa Kernel tank ye! [exits, after procession of Negroes etc. singing]

SERV. Now mother, I must be off!

MRS. S. At once?

SERV. Without a moments delay. Good bye mother-- Good bye darling. [to B.] Come let us hurry! [exits with BROWN, who lifts hat and coughs, r.2]

MRS. S. Lily--There is some new mischief a-foot--I can see it in your father's face--Ah, I wish we had never come to this unhappy land! [exeunt]

BURL. [enter r.2] Well--Here I am again! Can't keep away from the fire. She's yonder waiting on those little niggers--Well hang it, I must see her, in spite of them--so here goes! [exit l.] [music; lights down. enter r. BILL, SAM & JIM]

SAM. They're in thar treatin' the niggers!

BILL. Yes the derned Yankee's tryin' to put the niggers over the white folks, an' we're a dog-goned set o' cowards to stand it!

SAM. He ought to be taught a lesson!

BILL. Let's give it him now. Let's lay fer him here,

51

an' when he comes out, we'll give him a thrashing!

JIM. Better look out--He won't stan' no foolin'!

SAM. An' he's got your revolver too, Bill!

BILL. Sho--We're three to one--ef wust comes to
wust! [draws knife] This ull fix him an' won't
make no noise nuther--I can---Pst--Keep quiet--
Here he comes! [crowd exeunt l.]

BURL. [enters from house l.]. No--I can't stand it
any longer. There she is waiting on those niggers,
like a servant of servants. This dose is too much
for me--I'm cured at last--I'll never come here
again! [starts to go. SAM strikes him with stick.
is knocked down. SAM wrestles with BURL., until
BILL stabs BURL. in back]

BURL. [turns with cry]. Villains! Assassins! [JIM,
SAM & BILL exeunt r.]

MAUDE [enters from house]. Oh, Mr. Burleson--
you've forgotten your whip!

BURL. [staggering to her]. Maude--Maude--I'm--
I'm--- [falls at her feet]

MAUDE [kneeling over him]. Mr. Burleson--John,
John! What is it? Heavens--He's killed! Help!
Help! John, John, speak to me, speak, or I shall
die! [enter MRS. S. and LILY from house. Tableau.]

CURTAIN.

ACT 2

Scene. Sitting-room at Warrington. Fire-place l.;
large window r. Doors l. 1 & 4e.; table c.; lounge
r.c. LILY discovered asleep on lounge. Music.

BILL [steals on r.]. There ain't none o' the Yanks
   around. Three weeks ago I thought I'd killed that
   nigger-lovin' Colonel--but I must hev hit the wrong
   feller; we'll git him this time though! [places warning on table c., against books] That'll skeer him
   I'll bet. He knows that the Klan means biz. and
   ain't a-goin' to stan' no nonsense nuther. It'll make
   him crawl to find that ar purty picter here in the
   buzzum uv his family! [going; pauses] Wonder who
   it was I hit t'other night. It's durned strange he
   haint never been heard on. I'll bet I hurt him--
   whoever he was! Hello! The Yanks purty gal--
   Asleep!
LILY [in sleep]. Wait Melville--Wait! Think of my
   father--Yours too!
MAUDE [off l.]. No Dennis--No one must see him
   now!
BILL. Hist--They're coming--I'm off! [exit r.]
LILY. Hush--They'll find us! [rises] Hark--They're
   coming--Go, go quickly! [wakes] Dreaming again--

Haunted even in my sleep by this terrible fear. Oh, why did I listen! [turns; sees warning; shrieks. DENNIS and MAUDE rush on l.]

DENNIS [xes r.c.]. What's the matter Miss Lily?

MAUDE [l.c.]. Lily my darling--what is it?

LILY [points to warning]. See-See there!

DENNIS. K.K.K. Be jabers--A letter from the Klan!

MAUDE [reads]. "Comfort Servosse--Beware--The Klan condemns you. Leave the county--within 3 days--or you'll be learned to stretch hemp!"

LILY. Oh, Maude that means death--certain death to my father--What shall we do?

DENNIS [coming down r.]. Och alanna--Lit's sind for the praste!

MAUDE. Nonsense--Let's prepare for the worst, and teach these wretches we're not children!

DENNIS. Be the powers we will an' this minit too! [going]

LILY. Where are you going Dennis?

DENNIS. Jist wait an' you'll see! [exit r.]

MAUDE. Oh--What a villainous outrage this Klan is, and yet it is said that men of the very first families belong to its ranks!

LILY [xes r.]. That's slander--cruel slander!

MAUDE. What if it were proved that even Mr. Gurney for instance was one of them. What then?

LILY. What then? Then I'd die Maude Bradley! [falls sofa r.]

MAUDE. Die! Can you not trust me. Tell me what

54

troubles you!

LILY. Oh, I cannot--I dare not!

MAUDE. Yet I know all.

LILY [startled]. Know all?

MAUDE. Yes--I know that you love Melville Gurney--
That his father would rather see him in his coffin
than the husband of a Yankee girl. That he dare
not face his father's wrath, and is wheedling you
with delusive hopes.

LILY [intensely]. No Maude--You don't know all. If
you did you--you--would never forgive me!

MAUDE [terrified]. Heavens--What do you mean?

LILY. My lips are sealed. I must suffer sorrow,
shame---

MAUDE. Shame--Merciful heaven!

LILY. Maude--My life is bound up with his!

MAUDE. What are you his wife then--Secretly his
wife?

LILY. Hush be quiet--See Dennis is coming!

DENNIS [enters r.; laden with guns]. Bedad--We'll
take care of the blackguards this time! [puts arms
on table] They'll find out that the worst Yankee in
the world is an Irishman!

MAUDE. Gracious Dennis--What are you going to do?

DENNIS. Uphold the ould flag and defind the faymales!

MAUDE. But if Mrs. Servosse sees this, she'll suspect the truth. Anxiety has already made her ill--
She must know nothing of this horrible warning.

DENNIS. Av coorse not. Nivver you fear Miss. If

she asks me questions, I'll tell her---

MAUDE. What?

DENNIS. Lies--an' plenty av 'em too!

MAUDE. Well then come Lily--Let us go to your
room! [going] Something must be done to end this
concealment! [exeunt l.]

DENNIS [putting guns in order; sings "John Brown."
ACHSAH steals on, howls on last line of song. D.
starts; drops gun on foot; howls]. Och--The divil.
Begorra its Axy.

ACHSAH. Yes a nice sojer yo' is. Pick up dat gun!
[looks round; produces lock of hair] Yo' see dat?

DENNIS [terrified]. Och alanna I do!

ACHSAH. Yo' promised yo'd help my ole Daddy when
he was in danger!

DENNIS. I did Axy--I did--bad luck to me!

ACHSAH. De time's done come--Dey's gwine ter kill
him!

DENNIS. Och murther--Is it the Klan ye mane?

ACHSAH. A lot of low-down white-trash. Dey's atter
him now. If dey kotches him dey'll hang him. He's
a hidin' out hyar in de bushes, wid some odder fel-
lers dey's atter too!

DENNIS. Och the poor ould gintlemin, bring 'em in
Axy--Bring 'em in, the whole crowd, and begorra
I'll defind 'em!

ACHSAH. All right--Yo' jes wait heah!

DENNIS. By the sod of Erin I'll arm the darkies and
if the Kluckers come here, I'll give 'em a taste of

56

my tactics! [sings "John Brown," enter ACHSAH
with JERRY and Negroes] Come in Uncle Jerry--
Divil a hair of your head shall the blackguards
touch while Dennis McCarthy's alive!

JERRY. Tank ye--Tank Massa Dennis.

DENNIS. An' what are the villuns a wantin' to hang
ye for?

JERRY. Dey say I'se killed Massa Burleson!

DENNIS. Oh, the liars! [laughs] Sure what a set of
fools they are now; how could ye kill him when---

JERRY & ACHSAH [seizing his arms]. Take care dar;
take care dar!

ACHSAH. Dere's niggers aroun'!

DENNIS. Yis bedad, I'll sware to that!

JERRY. Don' you member what de Kernel tole us
'bout poor Massa Burleson?

DENNIS. Av coorse I do--What was it?

JERRY. He said we misn't say nuffin 'bout Massa
Burleson, an' we promised we wouldn't!

DENNIS. That's a fact!

JERRY. An' we mus' keep our word ef dey kills us!

DENNIS. Oh, be the powers we'll not give 'em a
chance to do that. Look here, I'll just make white
men of these niggers in no time!

ACHSAH [laughs]. Golly Massa Dennis how yo' gwine
fer to do dat?

DENNIS. By givin' 'em arms and tachin' them to defind
the innocent. Ivery mother's son av 'em that's will-
ing to die fer the right, is white enough fer me or

57

any other honest man.   Here you, Sambo, Dick, or
whativer the divil yer names are--hilp yersilves an'
fall in!   [crowd take arms and form line back]

ACHSAH.   My golly, I'se dar too!   [takes gun; heads
line]

JERRY [laughs].   What won't dat funny Massa Dennis
do nex'!?

DENNIS.   Fall in--Shoulder arms--Right face &c. &c.
&c.!   [comic drill]

ACHSAH [down front; gets mad].   Sho--dis sham bizi-
niss is played out.   Whar's de powder and de bul-
lets?

DENNIS.   Oh be jabers, I'd nivir trust ye wid de likes
o' that!

ACHSAH.   Den how's we gwine ter fight de Kluckers?

DENNIS.   Sure we'll scare the brith o' life out av 'em!
The sight o' this crowd is enuff fer that.   It don't
take much to frighten a pack of cowards that hunt in
crowds for cripples!   Fall in now, till I tache ye
the charge!   [bus.]   Ready, present, fire!   [all
point guns; ACHSAH'S goes off by accident.   crowd
drop arms hide under furniture.   ACHSAH stands
trembling.   DENNIS recoiling in horror.]   Saints
presarve us.   The witch fires without powder or
shot.   Where's my noble army?   [LILY and MAUDE
enter l.   MR. & MRS. SERVOSSE r.]

JERRY [down l.].   De Kernel--Bress de Lo'd!

SERV.   What is going on here?

ACHSAH [starts with cry].   Hi dar.   Listen at dat!

58

[mob roar distantly off r. all listen]

SERV. What is it?

ACHSAH. Dat's dem; dat's dem! Dey's a-comin' atter my Daddy! [at feet of SERV.] Oh Massa Kun-
nel--sabe him--sabe him--Dey's comin' to kill him!
[mob nearer]

DENNIS. Fall in there--Fall in! [crowd present
arms r.]

SERV. [raising ACHSAH]. Get up Achsah and fear
nothing. No harm shall come to your father in this
house!

ACHSAH [kisses his hand; sobs]. Oh, tank ye Massa,
tank ye. De Lo'd bress yo'--an' bress yo'--an'
bress yo' fo' ebber an' ebber--Amen! [xes to JER-
RY] Oh, Daddy--yo's safe now--all safe--De Kunnel
says so, an' he don't nebber tell no lie--he don't!

BROWN [enters r. rapidly]. Colonel Servosse--Thar's
a big crowd a-comin' this way, an' I 'llowed one
more moughtened do much harm--'specially seein'
how mad the rest was!

MRS. S. What do you mean?

BROWN. Wal ye see they're lookin' atter young Burleson. They let on thet he's been murdered by the
niggers, an' they're out atter some on 'em now!
[mob roar. looks r.] Thar they come with young
Melville Gurney a leadin' uv em on!

LILY [starts; aside]. Melville Gurney!

MAUDE [supports her]. Courage dear courage! [mob
roar violently]

GURNEY [outside]. Order gentlemen, order. Justice
shall be done. The house shall be searched!

SERV. What--They dare to talk of searching my
house? [enter GURNEY, BILL, SAM and others]

GURNEY. Colonel Servosse, I regret to inform you
that a party of citizens of this county have come
here upon a most painful errand!

LILY [gets c.]. Is it possible sir that you dare to
enter my father's house at the head of a mob. I
thought you were at least a friend!

GURNEY. I am and more. It is for your own sakes
that I am here!

SERV. Explain yourself sir?

GURNEY. Sir, a great crime has been committed.
My friend, John Burleson has been murdered. Old
man Jerry Hunt, if he did not aid in killing, knows
the assassins. A meeting has been held and a com-
mittee appointed to take the criminals!

SERV. Well sir?

GURNEY. Having reason to believe that they have
taken refuge here, these citizens have determined
to search the house.

SERV. By what authority Mr. Gurney?

GURNEY. Fearing the culprits might escape, we have
come with no other authority than the determination
of the people to execute speedy justice!

SERV. Then sir you cannot search this house.

GURNEY. But sir consider. There are a hundred of
our people here--almost insane with wrath. It is

impossible for me to restrain them.

SERV. Then we will do it for you!

DENNIS. Yis--be the powers we will. Fall in there--
Fall in! [Negroes present guns. mob makes forward movement]

GURNEY [checking mob]. One moment! Colonel Servosse, if the crowd see these negroes in arms,
they'll raze this house to the ground!

JERRY [gets c.]. Don't hab no mo' fuss gemmen.
I'se heah an' ready fo' de tribulation ob de Lo'd!

ACHSAH [gets before him with gun]. No, yer don't
Daddy. Dey shan't tech you whilse I'se hyer!

SERV. [draws revolver]. Nor while I can pull a trig-
ger or give a command!

GURNEY. Colonel Servosse--I have a duty to perform,
and shall not hesitate--Do your worst! [advances l.

SERV. aims revolver]

LILY [knocks down his arm]. Father--Mr. Gurney--
For mercy's sake--For my sake--I beseech you---

GURNEY. My God--Must I recoil like a coward! [gets
r.]

SERV. Gentlemen--If you came here in the name of
the law, my house and all in it should be at your
service, but to the lawless violence of a mob, I
will never surrender a single inch!

BROWN [down c.]. Which reminds me, thet as I'm
a magistrate in this yer county, I've got something
to say. Ye've come here to take Jerry Hunt; hes
eny of you got a warrant fer him?

61

BILL. Sho now, that thur nigger's killed Mr. Burleson er helped ter du it, an' the peple of this county ain't a gwine ter stan' no nonsense about warrants. We haven't got none, an' don't wane none, nuther!

BROWN. You're a nice lot of law-abidin' citizens you are. Ef I done my dooty, I'd issue a warrant and arrest the whole kit an' bilin' on you myself! [cough] Ef it wasn't fer this derned cough--b'leeve I would. But seein' es how things is, I'll hev ter do the next best thing an' open a jestice's court right here an' give ye a warrant myself!

BILL. Now ye're talkin' squire. Jes' you make out the papers an' we'll sarve 'em, an' without eny cost to the county other!

BROWN. We'll hear the evidence fust ef you please-- Mr. Bill Sanders! Oh, yis--Oh, yis--Oh, yis! This worshipful jestice's court is now open to hear eny cases thet may be brought afore it! Hats off! [all uncover] The court's open, an' mind yer now, there's goin ter be order hyer. Jestice is jestice-- an'--wal you all knows Jayheu Brown!

DENNIS [aside]. Begorra--The ould gintlemin manes bizniss!

BILL. Plaze yer worship, I wants a warrant fer thet nigger Jerry Hunt!

BROWN. Wal what fer. What's yer charge agin him, an' whar's yer proof?

BILL. I charge him with the murder of John Burleson!

BROWN. Ye're mighty sure Mr. Burleson's been mur-

62

dered I reckon?

BILL. Of course, an' by thet nigger too!

BROWN. I suppose ye've found the body?

BILL. Wal no--we haint--But we've been er huntin'
fer it, fer a week!

BROWN. Ef ye haint found the body, how dy'e know
he's dead; an' ef ye don't know he's dead how ye
gwine ter prove he's been murdered--an' ef ye can't
prove thet, whar's yer evidence agin Uncle Jerry,
Mr. Sanders?

DENNIS. Answer thet ye spalpeen!

BILL [disconcerted]. Sho--I don't know wot yer driv-
in' at, but I know thet nigger killed him or helped
ter du it!

BROWN. But how'll yer prove it?

BILL. Why me and Sam Irwin hered Uncle Jerry
threaten Burleson, the day of the nigger blow-out up
here--the day he disappeared!

BROWN. Sho--Thet don't prove nothin'. I've heered
you swar to stop drinkin', over an' often--but yer
nose's better evidence en yer oath eny time!

BILL. But gol dern it, the nigger hez es good as confessed!

BROWN. Who to?

BILL. To Mr. Gurney here!

BROWN. Is this true sir?

GURNEY [rises; goes c.]. I fear it is sir!

BROWN. Hm--Things is gettin' serious. Ef thet's
so--what did he say?

63

GURNEY. Yesterday I tried to get him to tell me all he knew of Burleson. Once he forgot himself and confessed that something terrible had happened to him; that he had seen him afterwards. Then he stammered and after that refused to say another word!

JERRY. Dat's all true Massa Brown--De Lo'd forgib me!

GURNEY. When he heard he was to be arrested, he ran away and took refuge here.

BROWN. I didn't know the case was so strong agin you Uncle Jerry. I'm sorry, but I'll hev to give a warrant for yer arrest! [produces papers; sits table; writes]

JERRY. All right Massa Brown--I don't feah de law-- kase I'se in de hands of de Lo'd! [MAUDE whispers to SERV. who exits]

ACHSAH. What all is dey a-gwine to do now, I wonder?

DENNIS. The divil knows, but begorra I'm bustin' to shpake?

BROWN [handing paper to GURNEY]. That sir is the warrant an' I'll appint you special constable ter execute it!

MAUDE. One moment sir. The accused is here and surrenders himself to the law, but hasn't he the right to introduce evidence in his own behalf?

BROWN. Sartin' Miss sartin'--ef he's got any!

MAUDE. Then I propose to prove him innocent!

64

BILL. It'll take a derned sight o' witnesses to do
   that!
MAUDE. On the contrary, I'll call but one!
BILL [laughs]. Who is he?
MAUDE. Here he comes! [enter SERV. followed by
   BURL.]
ALL [amazed]. Mr. Burleson!
BURL. What is the meaning of this intrusion?
GURNEY [grasps hand]. John--Thank God for this
   hour--We thought you were dead!
BURL. I should have been but for the hospitality of
   this house which you have so infamously invaded!
GURNEY. But John why have you concealed yourself
   so long?
BURL. Because it was the best way to throw my as-
   sailant off his guard, and to expose him to discov-
   ery! [BILL starts] Everyone about this house was
   made to promise not to reveal whether I was alive
   or dead. Thanks to the faithful secrecy of these
   friends, convincing evidence has been obtained
   against this villain. He has been entirely thrown
   off his guard, and has even had the audacity to come
   here to help you arrest an innocent man for his own
   crime!
ALL. Where is he? Where is he?
BURL. [points BILL]. He stands there!
ALL. Bill Sanders! [SAM and JIM seize him]
BURL. Bill Sanders!
BILL. Hold on thar. This is a mistake. One word

with Mr. Burleson, an' ef he don't say so, you may
hang me on the spot! [shakes them off]

BURL. Well what have you to say?

BILL. Far play Mr. Burleson--far play! [aside] Ef
you caar to save the Klan you'd better hear me!

BURL. [starts; aside]. Save the Klan? What can the
cur mean? [aloud] Gentlemen--It's but right that I
should hear what this man has to say. Leave us
together a moment!

SERV. But he may attempt your life again?

BURL. No danger--I'm on guard now, and not in the
dark--Leave us--I know what I'm about!

SERV. As you will sir. Gentlemen please retire a
moment. Come mother--come Lily! [exeunts l.
with them. mob exit r. roar outside]

BURL. [to GURNEY]. Go--tell that howling mob that
I've been found!

GURNEY. I will! But John, I say--don't trust that
fellow for an instant! [exit r.]

BURL. Now sir! [loud roar from mob]

BILL [looks off r.]. Ef that crowd hears that I've
tried to kill, they'd jest tear me to pieces.

BURL. Well--What better fate do you deserve?

BILL. But I tell ye sir--I haint tried ter kill yer.

BURL. Don't lie. It won't help ye.

BILL. I don't lie. It was this durned Yankee Colonel
I meant to kill.

BURL. Indeed!

BILL. Yes--He struck and insulted me--and was tryin'

66

to set niggers over white folks.

BURL.   What right had you to punish him?

BILL.   Right! Wal as fer as the law is consarned
jest as much right as the Klan!

BURL.   [aside]. God help me--I never thought of that.

BILL.   Now I'm a Ku Klux John Burleson, an' I know
you an' a lot more of your friends ere too--I don't
want to do nobody no harm--but I'm a-gwine ter
fight fer my life. Ef you give me up to the law, of
course it'll go hard with me--I know that--but I'll
have my revenge--I'll denounce the hull lot on you
to the United States authorities.

BURL.   Fool! You have no proofs!

BILL.   Yes I have--I've got the letter Gurney sent you
tellin' him to meet you at Den No. 10.

BURL.   [aside]. Great Heaven! [aloud] Where did
you get it?

BILL.   No matter--I've got it--an' I mean ter use it
too!

BURL.   [throttling him]. Dastardly scoundrel!

BILL   [cringing]. Take car John Burleson--I'm a desperate man--an' I'll do jest what I say!

BURL.   [flings him off]. Traitor--as well as assassin!

BILL.   Call me what names you like--but jest let me
go ef you please!

BURL.   [xes r.]. And I and my dearest friends are
at the mercy of a wretch like this! [sinks crushed]
Oh what shame what degradation!

BILL.   Well sir--What are yer gwine ter do about it?

BURL. [starts up]. Do? Do what loyalty to my
friends forces me to do--Save the neck of a miserable cur like you! Oh, Gurney--Colonel Servosse--
Summon my friends! [all enter] Gentlemen--I regret to say I've made a mistake--I am certain now--
This man did not seek to kill me--I no longer make
any charge against him.

SERV. But sir--How do you explain?

BURL. Pardon me sir if I can explain nothing!

MAUDE [aside]. What can he mean?

BURL. And so gentlemen--I ask you to retire and
thank my friends for their anxiety on my account!
[exeunt crowd. to GURNEY] One moment and I
will go with you.

MAUDE. You are going too?

BURL. Yes, I must not remain another moment beneath this roof.

MAUDE. What do you mean?

BURL. I cannot tell you now! [exit]

BROWN [enters hurriedly]. Colonel--A boy jest
brought this ar fer you, an' from what he says I'm
aferd it's bad news.

SERV. [opens note]. A note from Judge Denton!
[reads] Great Heaven--hear this: "Walters has just
been killed--probably by the Klan--I go to investigate
the case at once. Come and assist me. Yours, in
rage and grief--Denton." Mr. Gurney--Do you hear
that?

GURNEY. I regret to say I do sir!

SERV. Well sir what have you to say of it?

GURNEY. I think sir that if sir northern men would
leave the south to work out its own salvation--such
acts would never occur!

SERV. Come Brown--We're wasting time. Mr. Gurney remember what I say--The day will come when
every decent man in the south will recall with shame
and humiliation the infamous deeds of this Klan!
[exits with BROWN and MRS. S.]

LILY [to M.]. Leave us alone one moment!

MAUDE. I'll be on the watch for your mother! [exit
r.]

LILY [looks around in fear]. Melville!

GURNEY. My darling! [takes her in arms]

LILY. Oh--How I have suffered!

GURNEY. Then let me end this misery and ask your
father's approval of our marriage at once!

LILY. Does your father consent?

GURNEY. Alas I fear he never will!

LILY. Then my father's pride will refuse to listen to
your prayers!

GURNEY. Ah--If your father and others like him
would not outrage every sentiment of my people--
my father's consent would be easily won--But things
grow worse and worse. The south determined never
to be ruled by niggers--has organized a Klan---

LILY. What--Do you justify this Klan?

GURNEY [embarrassed]. I don't know what you mean!
[goes l.]

LILY. Mean! I mean that if you justified that league
of fiends, I would rather die today than wear your
name!

MAUDE [entering]. Lily--your mother!

MRS. S. Come child--I wish to see you in my room!

LILY. Yes Mama--I will come in a moment! [exit
MRS. S. to GURNEY; aside] Melville--Forgive me
if I have said anything to hurt you!

GURNEY. Don't speak of forgiveness--I should beg
for that---

LILY. Oh Melville--If you love me---

GURNEY. Love you. Before another day has passed
my acts shall prove it better than any words. My
father shall come here to seek you for my wife--or
he and I will part forever! [pathetic music till
LILY off]

LILY. Oh Melville my husband. God bless you. [em-
braces him] I must go now--Good night--Good night!
[exits]

MAUDE. Mr. Gurney--I know your secret--and tho' I
deeply regret this concealment--I love Lily too much
not to be your friend! [extends hand. enter BURL.]

GURNEY [takes her hand]. God bless you for those
words! [kisses hand]

BURL. [angrily]. Sorry to interrupt your tete-a-tete
Gurney--but it's time that we were off!

GURNEY [going]. Let us go at once! [MAUDE turns
away proudly]

BURL. [starts; returns]. Won't you bid me good-bye?

70

MAUDE [indifferently]. Certainly!

GURNEY [aside]. I reckon I'm in the way--I'll wait outside! [exit r.]

BURL. Maude I'm going away--We may never meet again!

MAUDE [startled]. Why Mr. Burleson--You do not mean it!

BURL. Miss Bradley, I feel like a villain to have stayed here so long and let you nurse me like an angel without telling you the truth--but---

MAUDE [eagerly]. What do you mean?

BURL. No matter now--The past is past--In the future lies my hope. I have a terrible task before me but if I live to complete it, and return more worthy to ask you to be my wife! [pathetic music till off] If that day ever comes tell me that I may hope to win your heart?

MAUDE [turns; extends hand]. John!

BURL. [clasps her hand]. Enough--I ask no more-- I will come back a better man. Good bye sweetheart! [kisses her] God bless you and help me. [exits r.]

MAUDE [sinks chair with sob]. When shall I see his face again?

LILY [enters l.]. Maude--Dear Maude--What is it?

MAUDE [rising]. Nothing--nothing except that I'm so happy! [sobs] Miserable I mean!

ACHSAH [enters r. wildly]. Miss Meta--Miss Lily-- Miss Maude!

71

LILY. Why Achsah--Are you crazy?

ACHSAH. Whar's de Kunnel--de Kunnel--Tell me whar
he is quick!

LILY. Gone to Glenville with Judge Denton!

ACHSAH [laments]. Dar now--I know'd it--I know'd
it--I know'd it--He'll be killed--Killed!

MAUDE & LILY. Killed!

ACHSAH. Yis killed--Daddy here'd 'em in de bushes--
De Kluckers--Talkin' 'bout a party dat's gwine ter
stop de judge on his way home, dis berry night, an'
an' hang him--An' now de Kernel's wid him dey'll
kill him too!

LILY. Great Heaven, my father's life in danger. No,
no--He must--he shall be saved! [rushes to window]
Dennis--Oh, Dennis!

MAUDE. Lily--What are you going to do?

LILY. Don't ask me--You will see. Dennis--Dennis--
Oh, Dennis!

DENNIS [enters]. Yis Miss!

LILY. What horses are in the stable?

DENNIS. There's divil a one but mad Lollard!

LILY. Saddle him for me instantly!

DENNIS. For you? Mad Lollard? No, no Miss ye'll
be kilt intirely!

LILY. Dennis--My father's life is in peril! I must
reach Glenville in time to catch the train! Do as I
bid you--Go, go!

DENNIS. The Kurnel in danger. Och alanna--Murther,
murther. What'll I do? What'll I do?

72

ACHSAH [seizes him]. Do--Ye ole fool--Do as yo'
Missy says! [pulling him] De Kunnel mus' be
sabed!

DENNIS [xes himself]. Och awoo--Salve Pater Noster!
[exeunt]

LILY [xes desk r.; takes pistol out]. Oh, yes--It is
here!

MAUDE. Lily--What is that?

LILY. My father's pistol. If he is harmed this shall
avenge his murder!

MAUDE. Lily you are mad--crazy! The mad wild
colt will be your death!

LILY. He's my one chance to save my father. I'd
take that chance in the face of a thousand deaths!
[music till curtain]

MAUDE [seizes her]. No, no--This is murder--self-
murder!

LILY [struggling]. Let me go!

MRS. S. [off l.]. Lily--Oh Lily!

LILY [frantic]. My mother--Oh, let me go!

MRS. S. [off l.]. Lily--Lily dear!

LILY [struggling fiercely]. Let me go I say--I will
save him--I must! [flings M. to ground] I shall!!
[rushes off r.] [MAUDE unconscious. MRS. S. appears. Tableau]

CURTAIN.

ACT 3

Scene 1st. <u>Exterior of Black Rock Glen</u>. SENTINEL,
LIGHT, <u>and</u> 1st K.K. <u>discovered</u>.

1st K.K. Well comrade--any sign of the approaching
  camp?
SENT. None!
1st K.K. Let us enter the den and conceal our light!
  [exeunt. <u>Music till</u> LILY <u>well on</u>]
LILY [<u>enters l.</u>]. I thought I saw a light--but no--it
  was only some illusion of my brain. I shall lose
  my mind in this frightful place. My horse can go
  no further. The woods have grown so thick. Achsah told me to take the short cut to Glenville, and
  here I am lost, growing weaker with terror every
  moment, while death creeps nearer and nearer to
  the father I so love! [<u>signal off r.</u>] What's that?
  How horrible--My blood runs cold--Hark--I hear
  footsteps. [<u>the three re-enter from den</u>] Merciful
  heavens the Ku Klux! [<u>gets behind bush down r.</u>]
1st K.K. Are you sure you heard the signal?
SENT. Perfectly--As I watched the entrance of the
  den--I heard it twice before I called you! [<u>signal</u>
  <u>r.</u>] Ah--There's the signal again--from this side!

74

[xes l.]

1st K.K. Who goes there.

ALL [off r.]. Sons of the Empire!

1st K.K. Advance with countersign! [enter BURL.,
GURNEY, BILL and another in disguise. Bus.]
Brother commanders--the council is duly set--Who
bears the edict from the central den?

BILL. I--Commander No. 9 Pulaski County! [hands
paper]

1st K.K. [opens paper; reads]. Brother Commanders
--By this edict you are charged with the solemn duty
of executing the extreme penalty of our order upon
Jerry Hunt the nigger cripple and Thomas Denton.
Denton arrives by train at Glenville at 11 o'clock to-
night. You will intercept him at Bentley's Cross-
roads, on his way to his house--and then proceed
directly to the cabin of Jerry Hunt!

BILL. How far is it to Glenville station?

1st K.K. Four miles!

BILL. How far from the cross-roads?

1st K.K. Six miles!

BILL. Where is the shortest road?

1st K.K. One hundred yards on our left!

LILY. Ah--Now I can find my way. If I can only
reach my horse without being seen, I can save my
father. God help me--How am I to pass?

BURL. Comrades--We have an unexpected dilemma to
face. Colonel Servosse will be with Judge Denton
to-night!

LILY. My father's name!

BURL. He will never desert his friend. In this emergency the question arises as to what we shall do?

BILL. I move this camp serve Servosse the same as Denton!

BURL. One moment. As Grand Commander of Glenville County, I demand that this matter be discussed!

GURNEY. If this were my county--I should as Grand Commander interpose my authority, to prevent the execution of this edict!

LILY. My God--that voice!

GURNEY. We have no right to take the responsibility of another death upon our hands!

BURL. No--This edict should be referred back to the central den--with a statement of the facts!

1st K.K. It's cowardice to shirk the duty before us!

BURL. We have no command for the death of Servosse--and therefore no duty!

BILL. I claim a vote on my motion!

SENT. I second the motion!

1st K.K. All in favor of this motion say aye!

ALL. Aye!

GURNEY & BURL. Stop--We protest! [hands raised]

1st K.K. Order! Interrupt the vote of the Klan at your peril. All opposed to this motion say no!

GURNEY & BURL. No!

1st K.K. The motion is carried five to two--All discussion must end. We will now proceed to draw the lot of the executioner for Colonel Servosse! [pre-

76

pares box of lots]

GURNEY [aside to BURL.]. I cannot--I will not draw!

BURL. You must--or violate the oath of the Klan--
Face your chance like a man.

1st K.K. Now gentlemen--Draw! [presents box with
slips of paper. all draw] It is done--Approach
Light! Now to examine lots! Commander No. 7
Rockland County.

NO. 7 [advances]. Here! [presents lot]

1st K.K. Blank! Stand back! Commander No. 9
Pulaski County.

BILL [advances]. Here!

1st K.K. Blank! Stand back! Grand Commander of
Hilton County! [music]

LILY. Hilton County--Melville's home. Oh Heaven it
must be my husband! [sinks crushed]

GURNEY [advances slowly]. Here!

1st K.K. This lot bears the death symbol of the Klan.
On you, the Grand Commander of Hilton County, de-
volves the duty of executing Comfort Servosse!
[GURNEY staggers. LILY falls unconscious]

BURL. [supporting GURNEY]. Courage man courage!
[music stops]

1st K.K. Now comrades--If you will come with me, I
will show you the hospitality of the den!

BURL. We will await you here!

1st K.K. As you please! [to others] Follow me!
[exeunt omnes c.]

BURL. What are you going to do?

77

GURNEY. One of two things, I must kill Servosse or die. You can guess which I shall do, when I tell you that Lily Servosse is my wife!

BURL. Great Heaven--This matter shall go no further!

GURNEY. There is no hope--No one can escape the avenging power of the Klan. I must die or, ---

BURL. Or revolt!

GURNEY. Revolt! Betray the south?

BURL. No--redeem the south. When we made our compact with the Klan--its sole purpose was to frighten niggers from the poles, and so prevent nigger rule in the south. But the scum of our state have crept into our ranks, prostituting its power to murder for mere personal revenge!

GURNEY. What can we do?

BURL. Face and baffle those that disgrace our southern manhood. Follow my lead this night, and I will show you a way to stake your life--not for Servosse alone--but also for the deliverance of the south from the tyranny of these fiends!

GURNEY [grasps hand]. Lead the road and I will follow you into the jaws of death! [LILY moves-- moans]

BURL. Hark!

GURNEY. What is it?

BURL. Did you hear nothing?

GURNEY. Nothing!

BURL. Well then let us retire and I will explain my plans! [exeunt r. 3]

78

LILY [revives]. Ah, that light yonder--It is the Klan
--I remember--Melville my father. Oh if I can only reach my horse--I may save him yet. Let me
see--I tied him on this side--He can't be far from
the road! [draws revolver] Thank God--I have this.
Heaven steel my heart and nerve my hand--Woe to
the man that bars my path! [music till end]
BURL. [re-enters with GURNEY]. Well--What do you
say?
GURNEY. That I am with you to the last gasp! [LILY
creeps c.]
BURL. [sees her]. Ha--Who is that?
LILY. Stand back!
GURNEY [startled at voice, springs before her, she
fires, he recoils--she rushes off. BURL. springs
after]. Stop! My God--It's Lily!
BURL. Lily.
GURNEY. The flash of her pistol showed me her face!
[staggers--B. supports. four of K.K.s enter]
1st K.K. What does this mean?
BURL. My friend is shot!
ALL. A spy! Search the Glen! [start]
GURNEY. Stop--stop! There is no spy--An accident--
My own pistol--See--- [falls c.]
BURL. Great Heaven--Killed by her! [stoops over
him. Tableau as scene closes in]

Scene 2d. Flats in 1. exterior of Jayheu Brown's house.

BROWN [enters from house]. Sam Irwin! Sam Irwin!! [enter SAM. locks door] Thar's your way now--Jest travel and be peart about it too! [SAM starts] Hold on--Come back! I'm forgettin' somethin'. You're sure you an' Jim Smith can swar ye seed Bill Sanders shoot Walters.

SAM. Yes on the four o'clock road close by Walter's house when he was comin' home from meetin' last Sunday afternoon!

BROWN. Did Bill hev on his Ku Klux rig then?

SAM. No--We don't war it by daylight!

BROWN. Wal see ye don't play us no more tricks--dy'e hear?

SAM. It warn't nary trick sir!

BROWN. The last time the Klan met I made you lend me your rig, and I went in your place--Thet was at Den No. 9 Hilton County. Thet time ye told me the truth--but to-night the Klan was to meet agin, an' ye told me a lie. You told me the Klan ud meet to-night at Johnson's Fork!

SAM. Bill Sanders told me so, an' I reckon he did it to throw me off the track. The Klan must hev met at some other Den--the Black Rock Glen--like ez not!

BROWN. Sam Irwin--ye know I've got my grip on ye at last--Ye know I've got evidence agin ye, that ud stretch yer neck in no time--ef I war to give it to

80

the court. Now why don't I give it to the court?

SAM. Kase ye know I'll help ye catch a derned sight worse rascal then ye say I be--ef ye keep it out of court!

BROWN. Hm--Thar's some truth in that--But thar is mischief a foot to-night, and this Bill Sanders is at the bottom of it--thet I know. Now you jest take car you find his trail this yer night and put me or Colonel Harris on it, or to-morrow mornin' all the constables in the county will be a-houndin' ye!

SAM. But Mr. Brown---

BROWN. Thar ain't no use in buttin' me Sam Irwin. Nothin' but the fear uv quick death ull sharpen yer wits. Yer uv got a durned good nose fer mischief-- and ef ye'll jest snuff round enuff, ye'll find Bill Sanders rasin hell some whar afore mornin--so jest be off! [SAM starts] Hold on--Come back! This is what I forgot to tell ye. When ye strike the right trail--jest hurry to the head quarters of Colonel Harris--an' he'll let me know--Look sharp!

SAM. I'll swar I'll do my best but---

BROWN. No buttin'--durn ye--go! [SAM exits l.] Now--I'll jest walk round a bit--He'll be back afore long. Blessed ef I don't think we'll get our fingers on this kussed Klan ter-morrer at sun-up! [coughs, going] Ever since I got on it's trail--durned ef my cough ain't agittin' better--Reckon I'll bury the whole crowd yit! [exit. pause. ACHSAH appears dragging DENNIS. MAUDE follows]

81

ACHSAH. Dar now--Yo's heah!

DENNIS [gasps]. Yis--Bedad I'm here--but my brith isn't!

ACHSAH [panting]. Massa Brown lives dar!

DENNIS. Is that so--Sure it's a wonder he lives at all--anywhere!

ACHSAH. Dar's de do'!

DENNIS. Is it? I don't deny it!

ACHSAH. Wal den--yo' jes knock Massa Brown out!

DENNIS. Och sure I'd never dare do that--He might shtrike back!

ACHSAH. Yo' durn ole fool. Knock on de do'--an he'll come out hissef!

DENNIS. Av coorse he will--Why didn't ye say that afore? [knocks, repeats, calls] Mr. Brown--Are ye there? Mr. Brown--sure--ef yer out be civil and say so. Mr. Brown--Will ye shpake! The divil take him--He's no gintleman at all--He won't answer!

MAUDE. He may be asleep--But we must wake him!

ACHSAH [to DENNIS]. Yo' jes do like me, an we'll git him out mighty quick! [yells] Massa Brown!!

DENNIS [imitates her--knocks on door]. Massa Brown! [bus. of trying to out-yell each other. MAUDE puts hands to ears]

BROWN [enters coolly]. Thet's right go it--I bet on Axy!

ACHSAH [astounded]. Massa Brown!

DENNIS. Howly Moses. The witch brings him out widout openin' the door!

MAUDE. Oh Mr. Brown something terrible has hap-
pened--and we want your help!

BROWN. Yer can allers count on Jayheu Miss! [re-
moves hat]

MAUDE. The Klan are going to Glenville!

BROWN [quickly]. Glenville!

MAUDE. To intercept Judge Denton and Colonel Servosse! Lily has ridden off on Mad Lollard for Glenville Station to warn her father--but oh--that wild
colt will kill her before she can get there!

BROWN. Which way did she go?

ACHSAH. Short cut for Black Rock Glen!

BROWN. Damnation--That's one of the dens of the
Klan!

DENNIS. Bloody murther!

MAUDE. Merciful Heaven--What shall we do?

BROWN. Do? We'll save the Colonel and his gal too!

MAUDE. Thank God--Thank God!!

BROWN. I'll run to the station and rout 'em all out.
We'll start a special car for Glenville right away!
Dennis go fer Colonel Harris and hev him and his
men meet me at the railroad in double quick time!

DENNIS. Bedad I'm off like hot-shot! [exit l.]

BROWN. You Axy--get a crowd of niggers and find the
trail of Miss Lily at Black Rock Glen!

ACHSAH. Dar's a crowd at my Daddy's a-shuckin'
co'n--I'll jes' hurry up dar an' start 'em off! [go-
ing]

83

MAUDE. Stop Axy--I'll go with you--I'll find Lily
Servosse--alive or dead! [exits with her]
BROWN. Now fer the camp--An' the trail uv this
Klan! [exit r. scene changes]

Scene 3d. [exterior of JERRY's cabin in mountains.
Cabin r. Corner of log-barn up l. rocks in back-
ground. trees r. & l. romantic mountain backing.
moonlight. corn in piles baskets. JERRY and NE-
GROES discovered shucking and singing. jubilee business, ending up with fast break-down by omnes. at
climax of dance, ACHSAH rushes in madly--followed
by MAUDE]

ACHSAH. De Kluckers--De Ku Kluckers! [NEGROES
shriek and shrink to each side] De Kluckers--De
Kluckers I say--Don't ye heah?
JERRY. Dar--Dar Chile--Hush up--an' tell us what yo'
mean?
ACHSAH. De Kluckers is a-ridin' to-night--Dey's at-
ter de Kunnel--Kunnel S'vosse!
ALL. Oh, Lo'd!
MAUDE. Yes Uncle Jerry--The Ku Klux are after
Colonel Servosse. Lily started for Glenville to warn
him. She's gone by Black Rock Glen. The Klan
meet there--They'll kill her too!
JERRY. What--Miss Lily dar--Oh, Lo'd--Hev marcy.
No, no--She mus be sabed! Chillun--Miss Lily dat
has been so good to yo' dat has gib yo food when ye

84

was hungry, an clo's when ye was cold, kind words
when ye sad, dat bress'd chile of de Lo'd is in
danger ob de Ku Klux--What is yer gwine ter do?
ALL. Sabe her! Sabe her! [pick up hoes--axes &c.]
JERRY. Dat's right chillun--De Lo'd will bress yo all!
ACHSAH. Jes follow me, an I'll get ye dar double
quick! [exeunt NEGROES l.]
MAUDE. [xes r.]. Now Achsah--Come--Let us go!
JERRY [strange cry]. Stop! Stop! [music]
ACHSAH [catches MAUDE's arm--points to JERRY].
De Lo'd sabe us--Look dar!
JERRY. I sees it, I sees it--De day am a breakin!
ACHSAH. I know'd it, I know'd it--De spells on him!
JERRY. Dar dey go--Dere hands is red wid blood.
Ha--Look dar--He's a-comin--a-comin dis way. It's
de Lo'd wid a swo'd--A swo'd burnin' like a coal!
[in terror] No, no--hab marcy Lo'd--hab marcy!
[shrinks back] No, no--spare em--spare em--dey
knows not what dey does! [ACHSAH and MAUDE
support him] See--Who's dar. That you Hulda--
My wife--my bressed wife. Why honey dey tole me
yo' was dead--but no--it's only sin dat dies--only
sin dat dies! [sinks back unconscious. music stops]
ACHSAH [feels his face]. Oh Lo'd! Oh Lo'd! [starts
with cry] He's dead--He's dead--My Daddy's dead!
MAUDE [feels his heart]. Hush child--His heart still
beats. Run Achsah--Run for help.
ACHSAH. Whar--Whar--Oh, whar?
MAUDE. For the doctor--Mr. Burleson--Mr. Brown--

85

Anybody. If you would save his life--go at once!

ACHSAH. Sabe him--Sabe him--Oh I'll go like de wind on de water! [exit]

MAUDE [takes off shawl, places in under his head]. Poor old man. There--He will be more comfortable so. Let me see--What can I do. Water--yes-- some water may revive him. There may be some in the house! [exit. BILL as K.K. enters r. 4 with another who has a rope. MAUDE returns with cup, puts it to JERRY's lips] Oh thank Heaven, he revives. There--Uncle Jerry--do you feel better? [music]

JERRY. Yo' hea' Miss Maude?

MAUDE. Yes Uncle Jerry--Taking care of you!

JERRY. Yes, yes--I knows now--but whar's Achsah? [BILL gets behind MAUDE]

MAUDE. She'll be back soon!

JERRY. But how yo come hea' chile at dis time in de night?

MAUDE. I came here to--- [BILL places hand on her shoulder. M. turns gets c. with scream. JERRY falls prone. music stops. BILL beckons companion to go to JERRY] Ah Heaven I see you mean to kill him! [gets in front of JERRY] No, no--You shall not--You shall not! [forces BILL down l. BILL motions her to stand back.] No--I will not stir-- No man that is a man will lay his hand in violence upon a woman. I stand here to protect his age with my sex! [music. BILL beckons ROPE to go to her

86

ROPE starts. MAUDE stops him with beseeching
gesture. ROPE turns to BILL. BILL makes gesture of question. ROPE shakes head. BILL
snatches rope from him--struggles with MAUDE.]
Coward--Wretch Fiend!! [BURL. enters c., frees
MAUDE, flings BILL l. music stops] Oh sir--I
don't know who you are--but in spite of the vile
livery you wear--you must be a man! [BURL.
tears off mask. MAUDE recoils face in hands]
John Burleson!! [BILL beckons. Twelve K.K.s
enter l. 2 & 3]

BURL. That's right--Approach night-hawks and hear
me. I break the silence of our order as I break
forever the bonds that bind me in crime with you.
[Klan draw revolvers]

MAUDE [gets before him]. Oh--Have mercy!

BURL. [puts her aside]. No--No mercy for me.
Alive or dead I mean to rid my country of this infamous Klan! [Klan retire a pace] We've had
enough of this sneaking work. The south that fought
so nobly on the field is disgraced by such a crowd
as this. I loathe myself to think I ever joined your
ranks! [Klan point revolvers--advance a pace with
growl] Do your worst assassins. Kill me if you
dare--You dare not--You know John Burleson's death
will awake rebellion in your ranks! [Klan recoil
three paces] Do your worst then--Whatever comes
--your days are numbered! [Klan spring at him
with wild yell. Pistol shots off r.]

87

ACHSAH [rushing in]. De sojers! De sojers!

BILL. The Yanks!! Run boys run!! [exits l. with Klan quickly. ACHSAH lifts JERRY up. shots nearer.]

MAUDE. The soldiers--They're coming here. They'll see you--Arrest you as one of the Klan!

BURL. Let them come! [music till end]

MAUDE. No--No--They will disgrace--kill you perhaps. Oh, fly--fly!

BURL. That's something John Burleson never did!

MAUDE. Then if you won't save yourself--save me!

BURL. Save you?

MAUDE. Yes--The shame that falls on you, must cover me as well!

BURL. What--You forgive--love me then? [BROWN enters back]

MAUDE. I would rather die than witness your disgrace. Is that not enough?

BURL. Yes--Enough to make a coward of a God. For your sake I will go! [turns]

BROWN [advances]. Halt! [soldiers appear behind] In the name of the law--John Burleson I arrest you as one of the Klan!

MAUDE. No--No--No, No!! [faints in BURL.'s arms as---]

CURTAIN.

ACT 4

Scene. <u>Same as Act 2</u>. BROWN <u>and</u> SERVOSSE <u>dis-</u>
<u>covered</u>.

BROWN. Wal ye see Kunnel that this feller Sanders
is a durned slippery cuss. I thought I had him four
or five times, durin' the last three weeks--but I
was like the Dutchman who tried to catch the flea--
I put my finger on him--but he wasn't thar!

SERV. [<u>laughs</u>]. Well what chance have you to catch
him now?

BROWN. Wal as he's a durned dangerous sort uv in-
sect--eny man kin ketch him ef he gits a chance.
Jest keep yer eye open Kunnel an' ef he turns up
hereabouts--jest nab him short and sharp.

SERV. You can count on me to secure him if I cross
his path.

BROWN. Yes I can and I do Kunnel--An so good
morning.

SERV. And so good day Mr. Brown and good luck.

BROWN. [<u>returning</u>]. Oh by the way Kunnel--I'm forgettin somethin. [<u>opens bag</u>] While I was in a
neighborin state t'other day, I diskivered one uv the
rigs that the Klan wears thar--It's a durned sight

worse rig than our home-made Ku Klux here--so I
jest got one on 'em fer you as a curiosity! [takes
costume from bag] Now look at thet. Isn't thet
enough to make the divil turn pale?

SERV. By George I should think it were enough to
make him blush!

BROWN. Wal yes you're right Kunnel--That's the genuine article--the genuine article--an' you can keep
it to laugh at when the crimes of this Klan are almost forgot--An so agin good mornin!

SERV. Let me hear from you if I am needed!

BROWN [returning]. Oh by the way Kunnel how is
Miss Lily to-day?

SERV. I fear she is not much better. Ever since
that horrible night when she saved my life--she's
not been strong enough to leave her room.

BROWN. Just give her my respects Kunnel, an' tell
her ef she wants to make an old kuss happy--she'll
jest give Jayheu Brown something ter do fer her.

SERV. [shakes hands]. Yes--We know how true and
warm a heart you have.

BROWN. Thank ye Kunnel thank ye and good mornin!
[returns] And by the way Kunnel--Haven't you noticed how much better my cough is getting lately?

SERV. I'm glad to say I have!

BROWN. It's all along of the Kluckers Kunnel!

SERV. How so?

BROWN. Wal ye know ever since John Burleson dared
'em all like the reckless devil that he is--and gave

himself up--a crowd of the Klan has followed his
lead an' confessed too!

SERV. Yes thank God--John Burleson's bravery has
ended the power of the Klan.

BROWN. Wal Kunnel every time a Klucker's come
and confessed--click--went a wrinkle out uv my
neck!

SERV. [laughs]. Rather a queer cure for a cough!

BROWN. Yes--Queer but sure Kunnel--And so good-
mornin! Ef they keep on confessin--I'll be gol-
durned ef I don't die a well man yit! [exit]

SERV. Dear old man--He's as amusing as he is good!
[sits desk]

MRS. S. [enters]. Ah father--I have news for you.
Lily is determined to leave her room to-day!

SERV. But is she strong enough for that?

MRS. S. Yes I think she is. I even hope she is getting better and yet--my heart is sick with fear!

SERV. Mother--I am assured that some secret horror
is gnawing at her heart!

MRS. S. And I suspect what it may be!

SERV. What do you suspect?

MRS. S. That Melville Gurney is to blame!

SERV. What do you think he has dared to trifle with
the affections of our child?

MRS. S. He used to come here often before Lily was
ill--He has not been here once since!

SERV. His father died suddenly--the day after Lily's
ride--That may have kept him away!

MRS. S. [weeps]. Perhaps--but still, I fear Lily has lost her heart to that man!

SERV. Then there is but one thing to do!

MRS. S. What is that dear?

SERV. Quit this place at once. But go--go back to Lily. When I have seen her I will talk to you again!

MRS. S. Yes dear--You are right. We must leave Warrington. Once away from here we may save our precious child! [exits. SERV. sits--hides face in hands]

DENNIS [enters]. Ef ye plaze sor--There's a queer looking cove outside that wants to see ye. He says he's got something very important to tell ye!

SERV. Show him in!

DENNIS. I will sir! [beckons at door] Here you yender--The Karnel will see ye! [enter BILL disguised as old man]

SERV. I am at your service!

BILL. I must see you alone!

SERV. Dennis leave us!

DENNIS. All right sor! The ould blackguard looks wicked--I'll kape within call! [exit]

SERV. Well sir--Who are you?

BILL. I'm the Uncle o' Bill Sanders!

SERV. Ah--The Uncle of the man we've been looking after for a month--The man who murdered Walters!

BILL. The man the sheriffs hev been a houndin until they've jest druv him desperate--tho he didn't murder Walters!

SERV. We have two witnesses who saw him do the shooting!

BILL. Yes--As one uv the Klan. But ef Sanders is a murderer so is Burleson and Melville Gurney!

SERV. What do you mean?

BILL [hands note]. Read that and yu'll see!

SERV. [reads]. 'Dear Burleson--Jack Walters the carpet-bagger is organizing the nigger-rule in this state with great skill. A council of the Klan is held to-night at the den that I command to determine action to be taken concerning Walters. Don't fail to meet me there promptly. We shall be needed--You know what for. Yours--Melville Gurney. " My God--And this man has dared to visit my house --to seek to win the affections of-----But enough of words--Action must be taken at once---[takes up hat]

BILL. What are you going to do?

SERV. Have this man Gurney arrested as accessory to the murder of Walters!

BILL. Hold on--jest a moment--ef you please!

SERV. Well sir--What do you want?

BILL. You're a lawyer and I hears you're a mighty peart one too. Now I want you to defend Bill Sanders---

SERV. Defend that scoundrel for killing Walters-- Never!

BILL. But ye can't perceed agin him, without perceed-in' again Gurney, can ye?

SERV. Certainly not!

BILL. Wal then now--You jest promise me one thing, and I'll hand over Bill to you myself!

SERV. What promise do you want of me?

BILL. Why jest this--That you won't arrest Bill until ye've arrested Gurney too.

SERV. If you will give us Sanders I promise without hesitation that Gurney shall be arrested first!

BILL. On yer honor!

SERV. On my honor!

BILL. Wal--I reckon that's purty good security--I'll trust yer--fer-- [takes off wig and beard] I'm Bill--myself!

SERV. [amazed]. Bill Sanders!!

BILL. That same parsecuted man. Now--What are ye going ter do?

SERV. [xing to window]. Have Gurney arrested instantly!

BILL. Ye'd better take keer Kunnel. Ef ye perceed agin him, ye'll kill yer own child!

SERV. Kill my child?

BILL. Wal--I reckon purty near it!

SERV. What do you mean scoundrel?

BILL. Thet ye won't never arrest Gurney--An' so won't never arrest me!

SERV. I shall have him arrested before another day is past!

BILL [laughs]. What--Send yer own son-in-law to

jail?

SERV. My son-in-law--Why man you're mad!

BILL. Ef you don't believe me--jest go over to Hilton
County Court House--five miles from here and ye
can see the record of the marriage thar!

SERV. [aside]. Can it be possible that man has
dared---

MRS. S. [outside]. There my darling--You're almost
as strong as ever!

LILY [outside]. Oh how good it is--to get out of my
room again!

SERV. Take care--They're coming--Put on your disguise! [sinks sofa, face in hands]

BILL [puts on disguise]. Thet's right Kunnel--I like
to see you lookin' atter me so kindly--I won't forget
it. Thar--Bill's Uncle's ready ter be interduced!
[music till LILY c.]

LILY [enters with MRS. S.]. Father! [SERV. rises,
back turned to hide emotion] Why I thought you
would be glad to see me!

SERV. [xes to her]. Sit down child--sit down! I
have business with this man--I must go!

LILY. And leave me so soon?

SERV. Yes to prove----

MRS. S. What dear--More trouble?

SERV. Yes--I fear the worst a father can endure---

LILY [rises quickly]. Father--What are you saying?

SERV. God help me--I don't know--Don't mind me--
I'm doubtless frightened at false fire! [embraces

95

her] Good bye my child--I'll return soon, and
then----

LILY. Well?

SERV. Then I hope to have the right to take you forever from this place! [to BILL] Come--Show me
this record if you can! [exit r.]

BILL. By gad--that gal's pale face ull save us yit!
[exit r.]

LILY. Oh, mother--I---

MRS. S. Heavens my darling--What is it? My child
what can it be?

LILY. Fear! A sickening fear---

MRS. S. What dear? [music]

LILY. No matter now. Oh--How kind every one is to
me--and yet how little I deserve your love.

MRS. S. Derserve it my angel--Yes indeed you do--
All that any heart can hold or give!

LILY. Ah--But if you knew?

MRS. S. Well?

LILY. What hopes I---But no--It's nothing now--but a
wretched, wretched dream, that's past away forever!
[music stops]

DENNIS [enters]. Ah--Miss Lily--are ye there. Well
now God bless the day that sees ye smilin on us
once agin! Sure here's Axy outside wanting to know
ef ye'll see her?

LILY. Certainly--Right away!

DENNIS [beckons]. Axy--Axy--Ye may come in girl!

ACHSAH [enters with bag of potatoes on shoulder.

96

sees LILY, drops bag. falls on knees at her feet
in joy. kisses and fondles her hand]. Oh Miss
Lily--de Lo'd be praised--I'se in heaven now to see
yo dea sweet face out hea again! [dances about with
yell] I'se so happy--dat it tickles--tickles! [all
laugh] Sho--Yo needn't laugh! [cuts caper] I'se de
happiest gal in all dis world!

DENNIS. Yis be jabers and the spryest wid your legs
too! [picks up bag] What's this?

ACHSAH. Hi dar--Drop dat bag!

DENNIS [drops it]. I will Axy--I will!

ACHSAH. Jes mind what yo's about--Dat's my Daddy's
present to de Missy! [bus with DENNIS--xes to
LILY] Missy--hea's a bag of jest de biggest taturs
dat ebber growed in mud. Daddy an I raised em
jes fo yo to eat 'em an grow as fat--as de taturs
dairselbes!

LILY. Oh--Thank you Achsah. Dear me--If I were to
eat all those--I think I should grow fat indeed!

MRS. S. Achsah--She shall have some of these for
her dinner--this very day! Here Dennis--Take these
to the kitchen! [DENNIS lays hand on bag]

ACHSAH. Hi dar! [comic bus.] No ye don't--I jes
take dem to de cook mysef! I'd jes be a fool to
trus' a Ishman wid taturs! [exits r. laughing]

LILY [points outside]. Oh--see mother. See how
lovely it is out there--I wish I could have a walk!

DENNIS. An' why shouldn't ye Miss--Sure it's as
warm as tho it were summer. Bedad I niver liked

97

the topsy-turvy old climate before!

MRS. S. Yes--dear yes--It may do you good--We will go at once! [music till LILY off]

LILY [rises--walks]. See--See how fast I'm getting strong!

MRS. S. God grant you'll soon be well enough to leave this place forever!

LILY [pauses]. Leave this place--Yes, and the sooner the better. [exnt.]

DENNIS. Now to find that witch Axy! Oh--If I could only get back that lock uv me hair! [turns--sees costume] Howly murther--What's this? A Ku Klux rig as I'm alive. Will thin I niver saw one like this afore!

ACHSAH [off l.]. Dat's all right--I'll jes tell de Missy mysef!

DENNIS. Bedad--Axy's comin--Oh be the powers o' light--I've got it--I'll jest jump into this rig and frighten the witch! [gets into it] Yis--begorra an make her give up that lock uv me hair. Now thin I'll tache her a stip, she niver danced afore! [ACH-SAH enters dancing and singing. DENNIS gets before her]

ACHSAH [terror-stricken]. Oh Lo'd hab marcy-- What's dat?

DENNIS [deep voice]. The divil himself!

ACHSAH. Oh my golly! [starts]

DENNIS [stops her]. Sha--kape still!

ACHSAH [trembling]. Oh, Lo'd--Oh, Lo'd!!

98

DENNIS. Whisht! Whisht!

ACHSAH. I will Massa--I will!

DENNIS. Ye know Dennis MacCarthy?

ACHSAH. Dat durn ole I-ish fool?

DENNIS. Ha-Ha--Take care!

ACHSAH [starts]. I will Massa--I will!

DENNIS. Ye stole a lock of Dennis's hair!

ACHSAH. I did--Massa--I did!

DENNIS. An' ye tried to witch him too? [ACHSAH after pause--laughs] C-r-r-ck--Look out!

ACHSAH. I will Massa--I will!

DENNIS. Where's that lock uv hair?

ACHSAH. Hea--Massa--Hea!

DENNIS. There now--Ye've got ter do pinnince ye haythin winch--Dance fer the divil--dy'e hear?

ACHSAH. Yes Massa--Yes!

DENNIS. Well thin begin--an' quickly too! [she dances] Fasther--Fasther--ye witch! [he dances too. she makes a dash to escape--crawls under table--he pursues. she overturns table on him, covered with debris. MAUDE enters r.]

ACHSAH [throws herself at her feet]. Oh Missy-- Missy--Sabe me--Sabe me!

MAUDE. What nonsense is this?

DENNIS [crawls up from table--woe-begone]. Oh-- The nagur she-divil!

ACHSAH [starts up]. What!!! Yo a foolin me? [starts for him] I'll jes scratch yo' eyes out!

DENNIS [catches her arm]. Hould on--Ye can't

frighten me now--I've got back the lock uv me hair.

MAUDE. What is the meaning of all this?

DENNIS. Sure it's nothing Miss but a game of take and give.

MAUDE. Aren't you ashamed to turn things upside down like this?

DENNIS. Here Axy--Help me to set things right. [LILY and MRS. S. appear window]

MAUDE. What Lily--out of your room and walking in the open air?

LILY. Yes and the air has done me good.

MAUDE. Oh Lily--How thankful I am to see you here again.

LILY. Mother dear--I want to see Maude alone a moment.

MRS. S. What dear--Secrets from me?

MAUDE. My secrets you know.

MRS. S. Oh--That's another thing! [kisses LILY] Thank Heaven--my child has none of her own. [LILY clutches M.s hand] Come Dennis--Come Achsah--I Want you inside! [exit l.]

DENNIS. All right Ma'am! [comic bus with ACHSAH as they exeunt]

MAUDE. Now my darling--What is it?

LILY. Have you heard anything of Mel---Mr. Gurney?

MAUDE. Nothing yet dear!

LILY. Think of his never coming near me while I've been ill!

MAUDE. Be sure he has never known of your illness--

100

and he lives forty miles away in another county--I
would have written him but you would not let me.

LILY. No indeed!

MAUDE. But why dear?

LILY. Because--- Yes Maude--I will trust you with
the secret that is torturing my heart--You remember the night I rode Mad Lollard?

MAUDE. How could I ever forget it?

LILY. That night I discovered that Melville Gurney
was a member of the Klan. He was one of a number that drew lots for the killing of my father--The
lot of the executioner fell to him--my husband---

MAUDE. Oh--How horrible!

LILY. Now you can understand why I want to go away
--Why I hope never to see his face again!

MAUDE. And yet Lily--there must be some wretched
mistake!

LILY. Oh--Why could he not have been as brave as
John Burleson? [BURLESON enters back]

MAUDE. Why? Because there is only one John Burleson in the whole world. It takes a long time Lily
for nature to make such a man!

LILY. How you must love him Maude!

MAUDE. Love him. No I don't--No woman can love
him--Not as he ought to be loved. Gracious! Think
of me an insignificant little nigger schoolma'am,
having the impudence to talk of loving that great,
big, brave, noble fellow! [BURL. sneaks back a
few steps]

101

LILY. And yet--I am sure that he loves you!

MAUDE. That's the only thing against him. I don't understand how such a man can be such a fool-- But then he is--and---

BURL. You're another! [kisses her]

MAUDE. How dare you?

BURL. I dare do all that may become a man--Who dares do more--must be a woman.

MAUDE. Oh you villain--Before Lily too!

BURL. Pshaw! Miss Lily--don't mind--do you?

LILY. Not in the least!

BURL. Shall I take another?

LILY. Certainly--Do!

BURL. I will!

MAUDE. Stand back--or---

BURL. Come--come young woman. It's time this nonsense stopped! [embraces her] You may as well submit! [kisses her. LILY laughs]

MAUDE. Oh Lily--How good it is to hear you laugh again!

BURL. By Jove she shall be the gayest creature in the world! [beckons] Come here and I will tell you why!

MAUDE. What is it?

BURL. A secret!

MAUDE. But Lily!

BURL. Shall hear it after you--- [to LILY] May I?

LILY. Why of course!

BURL. [aside to M.] Maude--Melville Gurney's here!

MAUDE. Good heavens--Where?

BURL. Outside--Waiting for a chance to see her all alone!

MAUDE. No--No--He must not come!

BURL. I say he shall!

MAUDE. But, ----

BURL. No buts--She nearly took his life--She must make that life worth living now!

MAUDE. What do you mean?

BURL. You shall learn all soon. But first tell her gently he is coming--While I go to bring him in! [exit]

MAUDE. Lily dear! [xing to her] The time has come for you to learn the truth--You must be brave and strong---

LILY. Strong?

MAUDE. Yes--Someone has come! [enter BURL. and GURNEY. music till LILY repels GURNEY]

LILY [starts up]. He!!

MAUDE. Hush--He is here!

GURNEY. My God Lily--You are ill!

LILY [puts up hand]. Excuse me sir. I must refuse to have any words with you! [going]

GURNEY. For heaven's sake tell me what this means?

LILY. It means sir--That I cannot receive beneath my father's roof--the man that would have taken that father's life. As much as I abhor the Klan, so much and more do I despise Melville Gurney--the Grand Commander of Hilton County, who drew the

103

lot that was to make him an assassin!

GURNEY. But will you not hear me?

LILY. No--Words are weak beside the memories of
that awful hour. Go sir--Do not pollute this house
with the presence of such a man as you! [GURNEY
bows--turns to go]

BURL. Stop--I think I've earned the right to speak!

LILY. You have shown yourself to be a brave and
noble man. If only he had done the same---

BURL. He did and more. He drew that lot--Resolved
to save your father's life or die with him. 'Twas
this man--whom you spurn to-day that you shot that
night!

LILY [crushed]. My God! [face in hands]

BURL. Yes--and he in the agony of his wound--by a
quick invented tale of accident--blinded every eye
but mine--and left you free of all pursuit to do your
noble work!

LILY. Oh Heaven--Can this be true?

BURL. Upon my honor--I declare it. But for your
shot he had stood side by side with me and staked
his life in defiance of the Klan. But your shot be-
reft him of his chance and laid him low for weeks
at the very door of death!

LILY. Oh God--What have I done--What have I said?
[extends arms] Melville--Melville--forgive me or I
shall die!

GURNEY [embraces her]. No, no--I have nothing to
forgive my precious wife!

104

MRS. S. [enters]. Lily--my child--What does this mean?

GURNEY. It means that in the madness of my love for her--I have done you a wrong. Fearing that some cruel fate might separate us both--I begged, besought her to become my wife--- [SER, BROWN--SANDERS disguised. DENNIS--ACHSAH and two OFFICERS enter]

MRS. S. Your wife?

GURNEY. Yes--My lawful wedded wife!

SERV. [removes LILY from him]. In name perhaps--but never in any other sense.

GURNEY. Colonel Servosse!

SERV. Not a word sir! Gentlemen do your duty!

[OFFICERS place hands on GURNEY and BURLESON]

LILY. What are you going to do?

SERV. Arrest these men as accessory to the murder of John Walters!

MAUDE. John Burleson an assassin--That is false!

LILY [xes to G.]. No--No--It cannot be that he has stooped to crime---

SERV. I hold the proofs here in my hand. A letter from that man to Mr. Burleson, showing they attended the council of the Klan, to get Walters put out of the way!

BROWN. Ef thet's your proof it don't amount to any sartin sum!

BILL [throwing off disguise]. Ef the letter don't prove enough--I ken--fer I was thar!

105

BROWN. An so was I!

BILL, BURL. & GURNEY. You!

BROWN. Yes--I went in the rig of that rascal Sam
Irwin, who is now in jail. I was determined to
break up the Klan--I heerd everything thet night--
an I kin swar thet Gurney as Grand Commander of
thet county, prevented the Klan from condemning
Walters to be killed! As fer Burleson--he warn't
thar at all--fer jest before the council met--this
man Sanders, stabbed him on this place! [BILL
starts up r.] So officers--ye may jes as well hook
yer fingers on ter him--es he's the man thet killed
poor Walters to gratify a private malice of his own.

BILL [struggles as they seize him]. All right take
me et you will and hang me too fer hatin Yanks and
nigger-lovin whelps like these. May the curse of
Judas fall on the traitors thet hev broken up the
Klan! [exits with OFFICERS]

DENNIS. The day that rogue is hung--I'll belave the
divil's dead!

SERV. [extends hand to BURL. and GURNEY] Gentle-
men--I crave your pardon--I have done you wrong
and learned at last that some of the noblest hearts
that live, beat beneath a southron breast!

BURL. Colonel Servosse--Thank God this day has
come--The day when we have learned that the whole
country is better than any part. That to be an
American is a grander thing than to be a northerner
or a southerner!!

106

CURTAIN.

[music]

APPENDIXES

Appendix 1

Original Cast of <u>A Fool's Errand</u>
First Performed at the Arch Street Theatre,
Philadelphia, Pennsylvania,
on October 26, 1881

John Burleson	Mr. Steele MacKaye
Colonel Comfort Servosse	Mr. Herbert Archer
Melville Gurney	Mr. Donald Robertson
Jayhu Brown	Mr. Harry Courtaine
Dennis McCarthy	Mr. J.F. O'Brien
Uncle Jerry	Mr. F.F. Mackey
Bill Sanders	Mr. John Gallagher
Lily Servosse	Mrs. Belle Archer
Maude Bradley	Miss Helen Mar
Achsah	Miss Louise Sylvester
Mrs. Metta Servosse	Mrs. Emma Courtaine

Appendix 2

Passages from the Novel:
A Portion of Chapter XXXV
and All of Chapters XXXVI and XLV

These passages are reprinted from the first edition of the novel <u>A Fool's Errand</u> (New York, Fords, Howard, & Hulbert, 1879, pp. 239-245, 246-256, and 335-348) in order to provide the reader with two examples of how the novel was transformed into a play. Chapters XXXV, "An Awakening" and XXXVI, "A Race Against Time" contain the episode which ends Act 2 and begins Act 3, Lily Servosse's night ride to save her father from ambush by the Ku Klux Klan.

Chapter XLV, "Wisdom and Folly Meet Together," sums up, to a certain extent, Tourgée's feelings about the south and presents a somewhat more pessimistic view than does the conclusion of the play.

Chapter XXXV

An Awakening

. . .

Mr. Denton, the district-attorney, whose letter to Comfort Servosse has already been given to the reader, had been elected a judge of the State courts, and had recently, before the period at which we have now arrived, been very active in his efforts to suppress the operation of the Klan, and punish those engaged in its raids. By so doing, he had incurred the hostility of the Klan at large, and especially of that portion with which the suspected parties had been actually connected. There had long been threats and denunciations afloat in regard to him; but he was a brave man, who did not turn aside from the path of his duty for any obstacles, and who, while he did not despise the power of the organization which he had taken by the throat, was yet utterly oblivious to threats of personal violence. He would do his duty, though the heavens fell. This was a fact well known and recognized by all who knew him; and for this very reason, most probably, it was generally believed that he would be put out of the way by the Klan before the time for the trial of its members arrived.

It was under these circumstances that the Fool received a telegram from Judge Denton, requesting him to come to Verdenton on a certain day, and go with him to his home in an adjoining county. It was seven

miles from Glenville, the nearest railroad-station, to
the plantation of Judge Denton. To reach it, the chief
river of that region had to be crossed on a long wood-
en bridge, four miles from the station. The Fool accepted this invitation, and with Metta drove into Verdenton on the day named.

The railroad which ran nearest to the home of
Judge Denton connected at an acute angle with that on
which he was to arrive at Verdenton. Between the two
was the residence of Colonel Servosse, six miles from
Verdenton, and sixteen from Glenville.

The train left Verdenton at eight and a half
o'clock in the evening, and ran to the junction, where
it awaited the coming of the northward-bound train on
the other road; so that they would not arrive at Glenville until ten o'clock, and would reach the river-bridge
about eleven, and the judge's mansion perhaps a half-
hour later. By previous arrangement, his carriage
would meet them at the station. Metta intended to remain until the train reached Verdenton, and bring home
a friend who was expected to arrive upon it.

Lily remained at home. She was the "only
white person on the lot," to use the familiar phrase of
that region, which means that upon her rested all the
responsibility of the house. The existence of a servile,
or recently servile race, devolves upon the children at
a very early age a sort of vice-regal power in the absence of the parents. They are expected to see that
"every thing goes on right on the plantation" and about

115

the house in such absence; and their commands are as readily obeyed by the servants and employees as those of their elders. It is this early familiarity with the affairs of the parents, and ready assumption of responsibility, which give to the youth of the South that air of self-control, and readiness to assume command of whatever matter he may be engaged in. It is thus that they are trained to rule. To this training, in large measure, is due the fact, that, during all the <u>ante bellum</u> period, the Southern minority dominated and controlled the government, monopolized its honors and emoluments, and dictated its policy in spite of an overwhelming and hostile majority at the North. The Southrons are the natural rulers, leaders, and dictators of the country, as later events have conclusively proved.

It was just at sundown, and Lily was sitting on the porch at Warrington, watching the sunset glow, when a horseman came in sight, and rode up to the gate. After a moment's scrutiny of the premises, he seemed satisfied, and uttered the usual halloo which it is customary for one to give who desires to communicate with the household in that country. Lily rose, and advanced to the steps.

"Here's a letter, " said the horseman, as he held an envelope up to view, and then, as she started down the steps, threw it over the gate into the avenue, and, wheeling his horse, cantered easily away. Lily picked up the letter. It was directed in a coarse, sprawling hand, --

"Colonel Comfort Servosse,

"Warrington. "

In the lower left-hand corner, in a more compact and business-like hand, were written the words, "Read at once. " Lily read the superscription carelessly as she went up the broad avenue. It awakened no curiosity in her mind; but, after she had resumed her seat on the porch, it occurred to her that both the messenger and his horse were unknown to her. The former was a white lad of fourteen or fifteen years of age, whom she might very well fail to recognize. What struck her as peculiar was the fact that he was evidently unacquainted with Warrington, which was a notable place in the country; and a lad of that age could hardly be found in a circuit of many miles who could not have directed the traveler to it. It was evident from the demeanor of this one, that, when he first rode up, he was uncertain whether he had reached his destination, and had only made sure of it by recognizing some specific object which had been described to him. In other words, he had been traveling on what is known in that country as a "way-bill, " or a description of a route received from another.

Then she remembered that she had not recognized the horse, which was a circumstance somewhat remarkable; for it was an iron-gray of notable form and action. Her love of horses led her instinctively to notice those which she saw, and her daily rides had made her familiar with every good horse in a circle of many miles. Besides this, she had been accustomed to go almost everywhere with her father, when he had occasion to make journeys not requiring more than a day's absence. So that it was quite safe to say that she knew by sight at least twice as many horses as people.

These reflections caused her to glance again, a little curiously, at the envelope. It occurred to her, as she did so, that the superscription was in a disguised hand. Her father had received so many letters of that character, all of threat or warning, that the bare suspicion of that fact aroused at once the apprehension of evil or danger. While she had been thinking, the short Southern twilight had given place to the light of the full moon rising in the East. She went into the house, and, calling for a light, glanced once more at the envelope, and then broke the seal. It read, --

Colonel Servosse, --A raid of K.K. has been ordered to intercept Judge Denton on his way home to-night (the 23d inst.). It is understood that he has telegraphed to you to accompany him home. Do not do it. If you can by any means, give him warning. It is a big raid, and means business. The decree is, that he shall be tied, placed in the middle of the bridge across the river, the planks taken up on each side, so as to prevent a rescue, and the bridge set on fire. I send this warning for your sake. Do not trust the telegraph. I shall try to send this by a safe hand, but tremble lest it should be too late. I dare not sign my name, but subscribe myself your

'Unknown Friend.'

The young girl stood for a moment paralyzed with horror at the danger which threatened her father. It did not once occur to her to doubt the warning she had received. She glanced at the timepiece upon the mantel. The hands pointed to eight o'clock.

"Too late, too late!" she cried as she clasped her hands, and raised her eyes to heaven in prayerful agony. She saw that she could not reach Verdenton in time to prevent their taking the train, and she knew it would be useless to telegraph afterwards. It was evident that the wires were under the control of the Klan, and there was no probability that a message would be delivered, if sent, in time to prevent the catastrophe.

"O my dear, dear papa!" she cried, as she realized more fully the danger. "O God! can nothing be done to save him!"

Then a new thought flashed upon her mind. She ran to the back porch, and called sharply, but quietly, --

"William! Oh, William!"

A voice in the direction of the stables answered, "Ma'am?"

"Come here at once."

"Oh, Maggie!" she called.

"Ma'am?" from the kitchen.

"Bring me a cup of coffee, some biscuits, and an egg--quick!"

"Law sakes, chile, what makes ye in sech a hurry? Supper 'll be ready direckly Miss Mettie gits home. Can't yer wait?" answered the colored woman querulously.

"Never mind. I'll do without it, if it troubles you," said Lily quietly.

"Bress my soul! No trouble at all, Miss Lily," said the woman, entirely mollified by the soft answer. "On'y I couldn't see what made yer be in sech a powerful hurry. Ye'se hev 'em in a minit, honey."

"William," said Lily, as the stable-boy appeared, "put my saddle on Young Lollard, and bring him round as quick as possible."

"But Miss Lily, you know dat hoss"--the servant began to expostulate.

"I know all about him, William. Don't wait to talk. Bring him out."

"All right, Miss Lily," he replied, with a bow and a scrape. But, as he went toward the stable, he soliloquized angrily, "Now, what for Miss Lily want to ride dat pertickerler hoss, you s'pose? Never did afore. Nobody but de kunnel ebber on his back, an' he hab his hands full wid him sometimes. Dese furrerbred hosses jes' de debbil anyhow! Dar's dat Young Lollard now, it's jest 'bout all a man's life's wuth ter rub him down, an' saddle him. Why can't she take de ole un! Here you, Lollard, come outen dat!"

He threw open the door of the log-stable where the horse had his quarters, as he spoke, and almost instantly, with a short, vicious whinney, a powerful dark-brown horse leaped into the moonlight, and with

120

ears laid back upon his sinuous neck, white teeth bare, and thin, blood-red nostrils distended, rushed towards the servant, who, with a loud, "Dar now! Look at him! Whoa! See de dam rascal!" retreated quickly behind the door. The horse rushed once or twice around the little stable-yard, and then stopped suddenly beside his keeper, and stretched out his head for the bit, quivering in every limb with that excess of vitality which only the thorough-bred horse ever exhibits. He was anxious for the bit and saddle, because they meant exercise, a race, an opportunity to show his speed, which the thorough-bred recognizes as the one great end of his existence.

Before the horse was saddled, Lily had donned her riding habit, put a revolver in her belt, as she very frequently did when riding alone, swallowed a hasty supper, scrawled a short note to her mother on the envelope of the letter she had received,--which she charged William at once to carry to her,--and was ready to start on a night-ride to Glenville. She had only been there across the country once; but she thought she knew the way, or was at least so familiar with the "lay" of the country that she could find it.

The brawny groom with difficulty held the rest-less horse by the bit; but the slight girl, who stood upon the block with pale face and set teeth, gathered the reins in her hand, leaped fearlessly into the saddle, found the stirrup, and said, "Let him go!" without a quaver in her voice. The man loosed his hold. The horse stood upright, and pawed the air for a moment with his feet, gave a few mighty leaps to make sure of his liberty, and then, stretching out his neck, bounded forward in a race which would require all the mettle of his endless line of noble sires. Almost without words, her errand had become known to the household of servants; and as she flew down the road, her bright hair gleaming in the moonlight, old Maggie, sobbing and tearful, was yet so impressed with admiration, that she could only say, --

"'De Lor' bress her! 'Pears like dat chile ain't 'fear'd o' noffin'!'"

As she was borne like an arrow down the avenue, and turned into the Glenville road, Lily heard the whistle of the train as it left the depot at Verdenton, and knew that upon her coolness and resolution alone depended the life of her father.

Chapter XXXVI

A Race Against Time

It was, perhaps, well for the accomplishment of her purpose, that, for some time after setting out on her perilous journey, Lily Servosse had enough to do to maintain her seat, and guide and control her horse. Young Lollard, whom the servant had so earnestly remonstrated against her taking, added to the noted pedigree of his sire the special excellences of the Glencoe strain of his dam, from whom he inherited also a darker coat, and that touch of native savageness which characterizes the stock of Emancipator. Upon both sides his blood was as pure as that of the great kings of the turf, and what we have termed his savagery was more excess of spirit than any inclination to do mischief. It was that uncontrollable desire of the thorough-bred horse to be always doing his best, which made him restless of the bit and curb, while the native sagacity of his race had led him to practice somewhat on the fears of his groom. With that care which only the true lover of the horse can appreciate, Colonel Servosse had watched over the growth and training of Young Lollard, hoping to see him rival, if he did not surpass, the excellences of his sire. In everything but temper, he had been gratified at the result. In build, power, speed, and endurance, the horse offered all that the most fastidious could desire. In order to prevent the one defect of a quick temper from developing into a vice, the colonel had established an inflexible rule that no one should ride him but himself. His great interest in the colt had led Lily, who inherited all her father's love for the noble animal, to look very carefully during his enforced absences after the welfare of his favorite. Once or twice she had summarily discharged grooms who were guilty of disobeying her father's injunctions, and had always made it a rule to visit his stall every day; so that, although she had never ridden him, the horse was familiar with her person and voice.

It was well for her that this was the case; for, as he dashed away with the speed of the wind, she felt how powerless she was to restrain him by means of the bit. Nor did she attempt it. Merely feeling his mouth, and keeping her eye upon the road before him, in order that no sudden start to right or left should take her by surprise, she coolly kept her seat, and tried to soothe him by her voice.

With head outstretched, and sinewy neck strained to its uttermost, he flew over the ground in a wild, mad race with the evening wind, as it seemed. Without jerk or strain, but easily and steadily as the falcon flies, the highbred horse skimmed along the ground. A mile, two, three miles were made, in time that would have done honor to the staying quality of his sires, and still his pace had not slackened. He was now nearing the river into which fell the creek that ran by Warrington. As he went down the long slope that led to the ford, his rider tried in vain to check his speed. Pressure upon the bit but resulted in an impatient shaking of the head, and laying back of the ears. He kept up his magnificent stride until he had reached the very verge of the river. There he stopped, threw up his head in inquiry, as he gazed upon the fretted waters lighted up by the full moon, glanced back at his rider, and, with a word of encouragement from her, marched proudly into the waters, casting up a silvery spray at every step. Lily did not miss this opportunity to establish more intimate relations with her steed. She patted his neck, praised him lavishly, and took occasion to assume control of him while he was in the deepest part of the channel, turning him this way and that much more than was needful, simply to accustom him to obey her will.

When he came out on the other bank, he would have resumed his gallop almost at once; but she required him to walk to the top of the hill. The night was growing chilly by this time. As the wind struck her at the hill-top, she remembered that she had thrown a hooded waterproof about her before starting. She stopped her horse, and, taking off her hat, gathered her long hair into a mass, and thrust it into the hood, which she drew over her head, and pressed her hat down on it; then she gathered the reins, and they went on in that long, steady stride which marks the highbred horse when he gets thoroughly down to his work. Once or twice she drew rein to examine the landmarks, and determine which road to take. Sometimes her way lay through the forest, and she was startled by the cry of the owl; anon it was through the reedy bottom-land, and the half-wild hogs, starting from their lairs, gave her an instant's fright. The moon cast strange shadows around her; but still she pushed on, with this one only thought in her mind, that her father's life was at stake, and she alone could save him. She had written to her mother to go back to Verdenton, and telegraph to her father; but she put no hope

in that. How she trembled, as she passed each fork
in the rough and ill-marked country road, lest she
should take the right-hand when she ought to turn to
the left, and so lose precious, priceless moments!
How her heart beat with joy when she came upon any
remembered landmark! And all the time her mind
was full of tumultuous prayer. Sometimes it bubbled
over her lips in tender, disjointed accents.

"Father! Papa, dear, dear Papa!" she cried
to the bright still night that lay around; and then the
tears burst over the quivering lids, and ran down the
fair cheeks in torrents. She pressed her hand to her
heart as she fancied that a gleam of redder light shot
athwart the northern sky, and she thought of a terrible
bonfire that would rage and glow above that horizon if
she failed to bring timely warning of the danger. How
her heart throbbed with thankfulness as she galloped
through an avenue of giant oaks at a cross-roads where
she remembered stopping with her father one day! He
had told her that it was half way from Glenville to
Warrington. He had watered their horses there; and
she remembered every word of pleasant badinage he
had addressed to her as they rode home. Had one ever
before so dear, so tender a parent? The tears came
again; but she drove them back with a half-involuntary
laugh. "Not now, not now!" she said. "No; nor at all.
They shall not come at all; for I will save him. O
God, help me! I am but a weak girl. Why did the
letter come so late? But I will save him! Help me,

Heaven!--guide and help!"

She glanced at her watch as she passed from under the shade of the oaks, and, as she held the dial up to the moonlight, gave a scream of joy. It was just past the stroke of nine. She had still an hour, and half the distance had been accomplished in half that time. She had no fear of her horse. Pressing on now in the swinging fox-walk which he took whenever the character of the road or the mood of his rider demanded, there was no sign of weariness. As he threw his head upon one side and the other, as if asking to be allowed to press on, she saw his dark eye gleam with the fire of the inveterate racer. His thin nostrils were distended; but his breath came regularly and full. She had not forgotten, even in her haste and fright, the lessons her father had taught; but, as soon as she could control her horse, she had spared him, and compelled him to husband his strength. Her spirits rose at the prospect. She even caroled a bit of exultant song as Young Lollard swept on through a forest of towering pines, with a white sand-cushion stretched beneath his feet. The fragrance of the pines came to her nostrils, and with it the thought of frankincense, and that brought up the hymns of her childhood. The Star in the East, the Babe of Bethlehem, the Great Deliverer,--all swept across her wrapt vision; and then came the priceless promise, 'I will not leave thee, nor forsake.''

Still on and on the brave horse bore her with

untiring limb. Half the remaining distance is now consumed, and she comes to a place where the road forks, not once, but into four branches. It is in the midst of a level old field covered with a thick growth of scrubby pines. Through the masses of thick green are white lanes which stretch away in every direction, with no visible difference save in the density or frequency of the shadows which fall across them. She tries to think which of the many intersecting paths lead to her destination. She tries this and then that for a few steps, consults the stars to determine in what direction Glenville lies, and has almost decided upon the first to the right, when she hears a sound which turns her blood to ice in her veins.

A shrill whistle sounds to the left,--once, twice, thrice,--and then it is answered from the road in front. There are two others. O God! if she but knew which road to take! She knows well enough the meaning of those signals. She has heard them before. The masked cavaliers are closing in upon her; and, as if frozen to stone, she sits her horse in the clear moonlight, and can not choose.

She is not thinking of herself. It is not for herself that she fears; but there has come over her a horrible numbing sensation that she is lost, that she does not know which road leads to those she seeks to save; and at the same time there comes the certain conviction that to err would be fatal. There are but two roads now to choose from, since she has heard the fateful signals from the left and front: but how much depends upon that choice! 'It must be this, " she says to herself; and, as she says it, the sickening conviction comes, 'No, no: it is the other!'" She hears hoof-strokes upon the road in front, on that to her left, and now, too, on that which turns sheer to the right. From one to the other the whistle sounds, --sharp, short signals. Her heart sinks within her. She has halted at the very rendezvous of the enemy. They are all about her. To attempt to ride down either road now is to invite destruction.

She woke from her stupor when the first horseman came in sight, and thanked God for her dark horse and colorless habit. She urged young Lollard among the dense scrub-pines which grew between the two roads from which she knew that she must choose, turned his head back towards the point of intersection, drew her revolver, leaned over upon his neck, and peered through the overhanging branches. She patted her horse's head, and whispered to him softly to keep him still.

Hardly had she placed herself in hiding, before the open space around the intersecting roads was alive with disguised horsemen. She could catch glimpses of their figures as she gazed through the clustering spines. Three men came into the road which ran along to the right of where she stood. They were hardly five steps from where she lay, panting, but determined, on the faithful horse, which moved not a muscle. Once he had neighed before they came so near; but there were so many horses neighing and snuffing, that no one had heeded it. She remembered a little flask which Maggie had put into her pocket. It was whiskey. She put up her revolver, drew out the flask, opened it, poured some in her hand, and, leaning forward, rubbed it on the horse's nose. He did not offer to neigh again.

One of the men who stood near her spoke.

"Gentlemen, I am the East Commander of Camp No. 5 of Pultowa County."

"And I, of Camp No. 8, of Wayne."

"And I, of No. 12, Sevier."

"You are the men I expected to meet," said the first.

"We were ordered to report to you," said the others.

"This is Bentley's Cross, then, I presume."

"The same."

"Four miles from Glenville, I believe?"

"Nigh about that," said one of the others.

"We leave this road about a mile and a half from this place?"

"Yes, and cross by a country way to the river-road."

"What is the distance to the river-road by this route?"

"Not far from five miles."

"It is now about half-past nine; so that there is no haste. How many men have you each?"

"Thirty-two from No. 8."

"Thirty-one from No. 12."

"I have myself forty. Are yours informed of the work on hand?"

"Not a word."

"Are we quite secure here?"

"I have had the roads picketed since sundown," answered one. "I myself just came from the south, not ten minutes before you signaled."

"Ah! I thought I heard a horse on that road."

"Has the party we want left Verdenton?"

"A messenger from Glenville says he is on the train with the carpet-bagger Servosse."

"Going home with him?"

"Yes."

"The decree does not cover Servosse?"

"No."

"I don't half like the business, anyhow, and am not inclined to go beyond express orders. What do you say about it?" asked the leader.

"Hadn't we better say the decree covers both?" asked one.

"I can't do it," said the leader with decision.

"You remember our rules," said the third, -- "'when a party is made up by details from different camps, it shall constitute a camp so far as to regulate its own action; and all matters pertaining to such action which the officer in command may see fit to submit to it shall be decided by a majority vote.' I think this

131

had better be left to the camp?"

"I agree with you," said the leader. "But, before we do so, let's have a drink."

He produced a flask, and they all partook of its contents. Then they went back to the intersection of the roads, mounted their horses, and the leader commanded, "Attention!"

The men gathered closer, and then all was still. Then the leader said, in words distinctly heard by the trembling girl, --

"Gentlemen, we have met here, under a solemn and duly authenticated decree of a properly organized camp of the county of Rockford, to execute for them the extreme penalty of our order upon Thomas Denton, in the way and manner therein prescribed. This unpleasant duty of course will be done as becomes earnest men. We are, however, informed that there will be with the said Denton at the time we are directed to take him another notorious Radical well known to you all, Colonel Comfort Servosse. He is not included in the decree; and I now submit for your determination the question, 'What shall be done with him?'"

There was a moment's buzz in the crowd.

One careless-toned fellow said that he thought it would be well enough to wait till they caught their hare before cooking it. It was not the first time a squad had thought they had Servosse in their power; but they had never ruffled a hair of his head yet.

The leader commanded, "Order!" and one of the

132

associate Commanders moved that the same decree be made against him as against the said Denton. Then the vote was taken. All were in the affirmative, except the loud-voiced young man who had spoken before, who said with emphasis, --

'No, by Granny! I'm not in favor of killing anybody! I'll have you know, gentlemen, it's neither a pleasant nor a safe business. First we know, we'll all be running our necks into hemp. It's what we call murder, gentlemen, in civilized and Christian countries!".

'Order!" cried the commander.

'Oh, you needn't yell at me!" said the young man fearlessly. 'I'm not afraid of anybody here, nor all of you. Mel. Gurney and I came just to take some friends' places who couldn't obey the summons, --we're not bound to stay, but I suppose I shall go along. I don't like it, though, and, if I get much sicker, I shall leave. You can count on that!"

'If you stir from your place," said the leader sternly, 'I shall put a bullet through you."

'Oh, you go to hell!" retorted the other. "You don't expect to frighten one of the old Louisiana Tigers in that way, do you? Now look here, Jake Carver," he continued, drawing a huge navy revolver, and cocking to coolly, 'don't try any such little game on me, 'cause, if ye do, there may be more'n one of us fit for a spy-glass when it's over."

At this, considerable confusion arose; and Lily,

with her revolver ready cocked in her hand, turned,
and cautiously made her way to the road which had
been indicated as the one which led to Glenville. Just
as her horse stepped into the path, an overhanging
limb caught her hat, and pulled it off, together with
the hood of her waterproof, so that her hair fell down
again upon her shoulders. She hardly noticed the fact
in her excitement, and, if she had, could not have
stopped to repair the accident. She kept her horse
upon the shady side, walking upon the grass as much
as possible to prevent attracting attention, watching on
all sides for any scattered members of the Klan. She
had proceeded thus about a hundred and fifty yards,
when she came to a turn in the road, and saw, sitting
before her in the moonlight, one of the disguised horsemen, evidently a sentry who had been stationed there
to see that no one came upon the camp unexpectedly.
He was facing the other way, but just at that instant
turned, and, seeing her indistinctly in the shadow,
cried out at once, --

"Who's there? Halt!"

They were not twenty yards apart. Young Lollard was trembling with excitement under the tightly-
drawn rein. Lily thought of her father half-prayerfully,
half-fiercely, bowed close over her horse's neck, and
braced herself in the saddle, with every muscle as
tense as those of the tiger waiting for his leap. Almost before the words were out of the sentry's mouth,
she had given Young Lollard the spur, and shot like an

134

arrow into the bright moonlight, straight towards the black muffled horseman.

"My God!" he cried, amazed at the sudden apparition.

She was close upon him in an instant. There was a shot; his startled horse sprang aside, and Lily, urging Young Lollard to his utmost speed, was flying down the road toward Glenville. She heard an uproar behind, --shouts, and one or two shots. On, on, she sped. She knew now every foot of the road beyond. She looked back, and saw her pursuers swarming out of the wood into the moonlight. Just then she was in shadow. A mile, two miles, were passed. She drew in her horse to listen. There was the noise of a horse's hoofs coming down a hill she had just descended, as her gallant steed bore her, almost with undiminished stride, up the opposite slope. She laughed, even in her terrible excitement, at the very thought that any one should attempt to overtake her.

"They'll have fleet steeds that follow, quoth young Lochinvar," she hummed as she patted Young Lollard's outstretched neck. She turned when they reached the summit, her long hair streaming backward in the moonlight like a golden banner, and saw the solitary horseman on the opposite slope; then turned back, and passed over the hill. He halted as she dashed out of sight, and after a moment turned round, and soon met the entire camp, now in perfect order, galloping forward dark and silent as fate. The Commander halted as they met the returning sentinel.

"What was it?" he asked quickly.

"Nothing," replied the sentinel carelessly. "I was sitting there at the turn examining my revolver, when a rabbit ran across the road, and frightened my mare. She jumped, and the pistol went off. It happened to graze my left arm, so I could not hold the reins; and she like to have taken me into Glenville before I could pull her up."

"I'm glad that's all," said the officer, with a sigh of relief. "Did it hurt you much?"

"Well, it's used that arm up, for the present."

A hasty examination showed this to be true, and the reckless-talking young man was detailed to accompany him to some place for treatment and safety, while the others passed on to perform their horrible task.

✱✱✱✱✱✱✱✱✱✱✱

The train from Verdenton had reached and left Glenville. The incomers had been divided between the rival hotels, the porters had removed the luggage, and the agent was just entering his office, when a foam-flecked horse with bloody nostrils and fiery eyes, ridden by a young girl with a white, set face, and fair, flowing hair, dashed up to the station.

"Judge Denton!" the rider shrieked.

The agent had but time to motion with his hand, and she had swept on towards a carriage which was being swiftly driven away from the station, and which was just visible at the turn of the village street.

"Papa, Papa!" shrieked the girlish voice as she swept on.

A frightened face glanced backward from the carriage, and in an instant Comfort Servosse was standing in the path of the rushing steed.

"Ho, Lollard!" he shouted, in a voice which rang over the sleepy town like a trumpet-note.

The amazed horse veered quickly to one side, and stopped as if stricken to stone, while Lily fell insensible into her father's arms. When she recovered, he was bending over her with a look in his eyes which she will never forget.

Chapter XLV

Wisdom and Folly Meet Together

It was shortly after the rupture of his home-life and his departure from Warrington, that Servosse visited, by special invitation, Doctor Enos Martin, the ancient friend who had been at first his instructor, and afterward his revered and trusted counselor. In the years which had elapsed since the Fool had seen him, he had passed from a ripe manhood of surpassing vigor into that riper age which comes without weakness, but which, nevertheless, brings not a little of philosophic calm,--that true "sunset of life which gives mystical lore." It is in those calm years which come before the end, when ambition is dead, and aspiration ceases; when the restless clamor of busy life sweeps by unheeded as the turmoil of the crowded thoroughfare by the busy worker; when the judgment acts calmly, unbiased by hope or fear,--it is in these declining years that the best work of the best lives is usually done. The self which makes the balance waver is dead; but the heart, the intellect, the keen sympathy with that world which is fast slipping away, remain, and the ripened energies act without the wastefulness of passion. It was in this calm brightness which precedes the twilight, that Enos Martin sat down to converse with the man, now rugged and mature, whom he had watched while he grew from youth into manhood, and from early manhood to its maturity. A score of years had passed since they had met. To the one, these years had been full of action. He had been in the current, had breasted its buffetings, and been carried away out of the course which he had marked out for himself on life's great chart, by its cross-currents and counter-eddies. He had a scar to show for every struggle. His heart had throbbed in harmony with the great world-pulse in every one of the grand purposes with which it had swelled during those years. The other had watched with keenest apprehension those movements which had veered and whirled about in their turbid currents the life of the other, himself but little moved, but ever seeking to draw what lessons of value he might from such observation, for the instruction and guidance of other young souls who were yet but skirting the shore of the great sea of life.

This constant and observant interest in the great social movements of the world which he overlooked from so serene a height had led him to note with peculiar care the relations of the nation to the recently subjugated portion of the South, and more especially that transition period which comes between Chattelism, or some form in individual subordination and dependence, and absolute individual autonomy. This is known by different names in different lands and ages, --villenage in England, serfdom in Russia. In regard to this, his inquiries had been most profound, and his interest in all those national questions had accordingly been of the liveliest character: hence his keen desire to see his old pupil, and to talk with one in whom he had confidence as an observer, in regard to the phenomena he had witnessed and the conclusions at which he had arrived, and to compare the same, not only with his own more remote observations, but also with the facts of history. They sat together for a long time in the library where the elder had gathered the intellectual wealth of the world and the ages, and renewed the personal knowledge of each other which a score of years had interrupted. The happenings of the tumultuous life, the growth of the quiet one, were both recounted; and then their conversation drifted to that topic

which had engrossed so much of the thought of both, --
that great world-current of which both lives were but
unimportant incidents.

"And so, " said the elder gravely, "you think,
Colonel Servosse, that what has been termed Reconstruction is a magnificent failure?"

"Undoubtedly, " was the reply, "so far as con-
cerns the attainment of the result intended by its pro-
jectors, expected by the world, and to be looked for
as a logical sequence of the war. "

"I do not know that I fully understand your
limitation, " said Martin doubtfully.

"I mean, " said the younger man, "that Reconstruction was a failure so far as it attempted to unify
the nation, to make one people in fact of what had been
one only in name before the convulsion of civil war.
It was a failure, too, so far as it attempted to fix and
secure the position and rights of the colored race.
They were fixed, it is true, on paper, and security of
a certain sort taken to prevent the abrogation of that
formal declaration. No guaranty whatever was provided
against their practical subversion, which was accomplished with an ease and impunity that amazed those
who instituted the movement. "

"You must at least admit that the dogma of
'State Rights' was settled by the war and by that system of summary and complete national control over the
erring commonwealths which we call Reconstruction, "
said Martin.

"On the contrary, " answered Servosse, "the doctrine of 'State Rights' is altogether unimpaired and untouched by what has occurred, except in one particular; to wit, the right of peaceable secession. The war settled that. The Nation asserted its right to defend itself against disruption. "

"Did it not also assert its right to re-create, to make over, to reconstruct?" asked the elder man.

"Not at all, " was the reply. "Reconstruction was never asserted as a right, at least not formally and authoritatively. Some did so affirm; but they were accounted visionaries. The act of reconstruction was excused as a necessary sequence of the failure of attempted secession: it was never defended or promulgated as a right of the nation, even to secure its own safety. "

"Why, then, do you qualify the declaration of failure?" asked Martin. "It seems to me to have been absolute and complete. "

"Not at all, " answered Servosse with some vehemence. "A great deal was gained by it. Suppose a child does wrong a hundred times, is reproved for it each time, and only at the last reproof expresses sorrow, and professes a desire to do better, and the very next day repeats the offense. The parent does not despair, nor count the repentance as nothing gained. On the contrary, a great step has been made: the wrong has been admitted and is thereafter without excuse. Thenceforward, Nathan-like, the parent can point the offender to his own judgment on his own act. So Reconstruction was a great step in advance, in that it formulated a confession of error. It gave us a construction of 'we the people' in the preamble of our Federal Constitution which gave the lie to that which had formerly prevailed. It recognized and formulated the universality of manhood in governmental power, and, in one phase or another of its development, compelled for formal assent of all sections and parties."

"And is this all that has been gained by all these years of toil and struggle and blood?" asked the old man with a sigh.

"Is it not enough, my friend?" replied the Fool, with a reproachful tone. "Is not almost a century of falsehood and hypocrisy cheaply atoned by a decade of chastisement? The confession of error is the hardest part of repentance, whether in a man or in a nation. It is there the Devil always makes his strongest fight. After that, he has to come down out of the mountain, and fight in the valley. He is wounded, crippled, and easily put to rout."

"You do not regard the struggle between the North and the South as ended, then," said Martin.

"Ended?" ejaculated the Fool sharply. "It is just begun! I do not mean the physical tug of war between definitely defined sections. That is a mere incident of a great underlying struggle,--a conflict which is ever going on between two antagonistic ideas. It was like a stream with here and there an angry rapid,

142

before the war; then, for a time, it was like a foam-
ing cascade; and since then it has been the sullen,
dark, but deep and quiet whirlpool, which lies below
the fall, full of driftwood and shadows, and angry mut-
terings, and unseen currents, and hidden forces, whose
farther course no one can foretell, only that it must go
on.

> 'The deepest ice that ever froze
> Can only o'er the river close:
> The living stream lies quick below,
> And flows--and can not cease to flow!'"

"Do you mean to say that the old battle between
freedom and slavery was not ended by the extinction of
slavery?" asked the doctor in surprise.

"I suppose it would be," answered the Fool,
with a hint of laughter in his tones, "if slavery were
extinct. I do not mean to combat the old adage that
'it takes two to make a quarrel;' but that is just where
our mistake--the mistake of the North, for the South
has not made one in this matter--has been. We have
assumed that slavery was dead, because we had a
Proclamation of Emancipation, a Constitutional Amend-
ment, and 'laws passed in pursuance thereof,' all re-
citing the fact that involuntary servitude, except for
crime, should no more exist. Thereupon, we have
thrown up our hats, and crowed lustily for what we had
achieved, as we had a good right to do. The Antislav-
ery Society met, and congratulated itself on the accomplishment of its mission, on having no more worlds to

conquer, no more oppression to resist, and no more victims to succor. And thereupon, in the odor of its self-laudation, it dissolved its own existence, dying full of good works, and simply for the want of more good works to be done. It was an end that smacks of the millennium; but, unfortunately, it was farcical in the extreme. I don't blame Garrison and Phillips and yourself, and all the others of the old guard of abolitionists. It was natural that you should at least wish to try on your laurels while alive."

"Really, Colonel," said the old doctor laughingly, "you must not think that was our motive."

"Not confessedly, nor consciously of course," said the Fool. "Real motives are rarely formulated. I don't wonder, though, that men who had been in what our modern slang denominates the 'racket' of the anti-slavery reform should be tired. I fully realize that a life-time of struggle takes away a man's relish for a fight. Old men never become missionaries. Being in a conflict of ideas, they may keep up the fight till the last minute and the last breath. Old men have made good martyrs ever since Polycarp's day; but they don't long for martyrdom, nor advertise for it. If it is just as convenient to avoid it, they prefer to do so; and in this case they certainly derserved a rest, and more honor and glory than they will ever get, alive or dead.

"It was our fault,--the then youngsters who had just come out of the furnace-fire in which the shackles were fused and melted away from the cramped and shriveled limbs. We ought to have seen and known that only the shell was gone. Slavery as a formal state of society was at an end: as a force, a power, a moral element, it was just as active as before. Its conscious evils were obliterated: its unconscious ones existed in the dwarfed and twisted natures which had been subjected for generations to its influences,--master and slave alike. As a form of society, it could be abolished by proclamation and enactment: as a moral entity, it is as indestructible as the souls on which it has left its mark. "

"You think the 'irrepressible conflict' is yet confronting us, then?" said Martin.

"Undoubtedly. The North and the South are simply convenient names for two distinct, hostile, and irreconcilable ideas,--two civilizations they are sometimes called, especially at the South. At the North there is somewhat more of intellectual arrogance; and we are apt to speak of the one as civilization, and of the other as a species of barbarism. These two must always be in conflict until the one prevails, and the other falls. To uproot the one, and plant the other in its stead, is not the work of a moment or a day. That was our mistake. We tried to superimpose the civilization, the idea of the North, upon the South at a moment's warning. We presumed, that, by the suppression of rebellion, the Southern white man had become identical with the Caucasian of the North in thought and sentiment; and that the slave, by emancipation, had become a saint and a Solomon at once. So we tried to build up communities there which should be identical in thought, sentiment, growth, and development, with those of the North. It was A Fool's Errand."

"On which we all ran, eh?" laughed the doctor.

"Precisely," answered Servosse sententiously.

"I am not sure but you are right," said the elder. "It looks like it now, and every thing which has happened is certainly consistent with your view. But, leaving the past, what have you to say of the future?"

"Well," answered Servosse thoughtfully, "the battle must be fought out. If there is to remain one nation on the territory we now occupy, it must be either a nation unified in sentiment and civilization, or the one civilization must dominate and control the other. As it stands now, that of the South is the most intense, vigorous, and aggressive. The power of the recent slave has been absolutely neutralized. The power of the Southern whites has been increased by exactly two-fifths of the colored adults, who were not counted in representation before the war. Upon all questions touching the nation and its future they are practically a unit, and are daily growing more and more united as those who once stood with us succumb to age or the force of their surroundings."

"But will not that change with immigration? Will not the two sections gradually mix and modify?" asked the doctor anxiously.

"Immigration to the South will in the future, as

in the past, be very scattering and trivial, hardly an element worth considering. There are many reasons for this. In the first place, the South does not welcome immigration. Not that it is absolutely hostile, nor intolerant beyond endurance, except upon political subjects; but it has been exclusive until it has lost the power of assimilation; and the immigrant never becomes part and parcel of the people with whom he dwells. His children may do so sometimes, but not always. The West takes a stranger by the hand, and in a day makes him feel at home,--that he is of the people with whom he dwells. The South may greet him as cordially as the Orient welcomes the Caucasian trader, but, like the Orient, still makes him feel that he is an 'outside barbarian.' Besides that, the South has no need for mere labor, and the material success of those who have gone there since the war has not been such as to induce many others to follow."

"But why do you think the South more likely to rule than the more populous and more enterprising North?"

"Because they are thoroughly united, and are instinctive, natural rulers. They are not troubled with scruples, nor do they waste their energies upon frivolous and immaterial issues. They are monarchical and kinglike in their characteristics. Each one thinks more of the South than of himself, and any thing which adds to her prestige or glory is dearer to him than any personal advantage. The North thinks the Southern people

147

are especially angry because of the loss of slave-property: in truth, they are a thousand times more exasperated by the elevation of the freed negro to equal political power. The North is disunited: a part will adhere to the South for the sake of power; and, just as before the civil war, the South will again dominate and control the nation. "

"And when will this end?" asked the elder man, with a sigh of weariness.

"When the North learns to consider facts, and not to sentimentalize; or when the South shall have worked out the problem of race-conflict in her own borders, by the expiration or explosion of a system of unauthorized and illegal serfdom. The lords of the soil are the lords of the labor still, and will so remain until the laborers have grown, through the lapse of generations, either intelligent or desperate. "

"Ah! my young friend, " said the old man, with a glow of pride in his countenance, "there you are coming upon my ground, and, I must say, striking at my fears for the future too. The state of the newly-enfranchised freedmen at the South is most anomalous and remarkable. I can not help regarding it with apprehension. There are but few cases in history of an enslaved race leaping at once from absolute chattelism to complete self-rule. Perhaps the case of the ancient Israelites affords the closest analogy. Yet in their case, under divine guidance, two things were found necessary: First, an exodus which took them out from

148

among the race which had been their masters, away from the scenes and surroundings of slavery; and, second, the growth of a new generation who had never known the ·lash of the task-master, nor felt in their own persons the degradation of servitude. The flight from Egypt, the hardships of the wilderness, the forty years of death and growth away from and beyond the ken of the Egyptian, all were necessary to fit the children of Israel for self-government and the exercise of national power, even without the direct and immediate interposition of divine aid and the daily recurrence of miraculous signs and wonders. Can the African slave of America develop into the self-governing citizen, the co-ordinate of his white brother in power, with less of preparation?"

"The analogy of the Israelitish people is so striking, that it seems to recur to almost every mind," said Servosse. "It is a favorite one with the colored people themselves. The only important difference which I can see is the lack of a religious element,--the want of a prophet."

"That is the very thing!" said the old doctor, with animation. "Do you know that I doubt very much whether there was any special religious element in the minds of the Jewish people at that time? They did not leave Egypt, nor venture into the wilderness, because of religious persecution, or attachment to their faith. Those were things which came afterwards, both in point of time and in the sequence of their growth and development. It was to the feeling of servitude, the idea of oppression, that the twin-founders of the Judaic empire, Moses and Aaron, appealed, in order to carry their religious idea into effect. The Israelites followed them, not because they were their religious leaders, but because they promised relief from Egyptian bondage. The instinct of the slave is to flee from the scene of servitude when his soul begins to expand with the aspirations of independent manhood. That this spirit has not manifested itself before, in our case, I think a matter of surprise; that it will come hereafter, I fear is a certainty. I can not see how a race can become prepared for absolute autonomy, real freedom, except by the gradual process of serfdom or villenage, or by the scath and tribulation of the sojourn in the wilderness, or its equivalent of isolated self-support, by which individual self-reliance, and collective hardihood and daring, may be nourished and confirmed. "

"They are likely to have their forty years, " said Servosse, "and to leave more than one generation in the wilderness, before they regain the rights which were promised them, and which they for a little time enjoyed. "

"Yes, " said the elder, "there is another dangerous element. They have tasted liberty, full and complete; and the loss of that, even in indirection, will add to the natural antipathy of the freedman for the associations and surroundings of his servitude. I very greatly fear that this unrest is inseparable from the state of

150

suddenly-acquired freedom; and that, animated by both these feelings, the race may attempt an exodus which will yet upset all our finely-spun theories, and test, at our very doors, the humanitarianism of which we boast. What do you think of it, Colonel?"

"Honestly, Doctor, I can not tell you," answered Servosse. "That such a feeling exists is beyond question. There is something marvelous and mysterious in the history of the African race in America, too, which appeals most powerfully to the superstitious mysticism which prevails among them. Brought here against their will; forced to undergo the harsh tutelage of slavery in sight and sound of the ceaseless service our nation offers up to liberty; mastering in two hundred years of slavery the rudiments of civilization, the alphabet of religion, of law, of mechanic art, the secrets of husbandry, and the necessity and reward of labor; freed almost without exertion upon their part, and entirely without their independent and intelligent co-operation,--with all this of history before their eyes, it is not strange they should consider themselves the special pets of Providence,--a sort of chosen people. This chapter of miracles, as they account these wonderful happenings, is always present to the fervid fancies of the race; and, while it has hitherto inclined them in inaction, would be a powerful motive, should it once come, to act in concert with a conviction that their future must be laid in a region remote from the scene of their past. If they were of the same stock as the dominant race, there might be a chance for the line of separation to disappear with the lapse of time. Marked as they are by a different complexion, and one which has long been accounted menial and debased, there is no little of truth in the sad refrain of their universal story, 'Niggers never can have a white man's chance here'."

"But what can be done for their elevation and relief, or to prevent the establishment of a mediaevel barbarism in our midst?" asked the doctor anxiously.

"Well, Doctor, " said the Fool jocosely, "that question is for some one else to answer, and it must be answered in deeds, too, and not in words. I have given the years of my manhood to the consideration of these questions, and am accounted a fool in consequence. It seems to me that the cure for these evils is in a nutshell. The remedy, however, is one that must be applied from the outside. The sick man can not cure himself. The South will never purge itself of the evils which affect it. Its intellect, its pride, its wealth, in short, its power, is all arrayed against even the slow and tedious development which time and semi-barbarism would bring. Hour by hour, the chains will be riveted closer. Look at the history of slavery in our land! See how the law-makers, the courts, public sentiment, and all the power of the land, grew year by year more harsh and oppressive on the slave and his congener, the 'free person of color, ' in all the slave States! I see you remember it, old friend. In direct conflict with all the predictions of statesmen, the thumb-screws of oppression were given a new and sharper turn with every passing year. The vestiges of liberty and right were shred away by legislative enactment, and the loop-holes of mercy closed by judicial construction, until only the black gulf of hopeless servitude remained. "

'I see the prospect, and admit the truth of your prevision; but I do not get your idea of a remedy, " said the elder man doubtfully.

"Well, you see that the remedy is not from within, " said the Fool. "The minority knows its power, and the majority realizes its weakness so keenly as to render that impossible. That which has made bulldozing possible renders progress impossible. Then it seems to me that the question is already answered, -- It must be from without!"

"But how?" queried the old man impatiently.

"How?" said the Fool. "I am amazed that you do not see; that the country will not see; or rather, that, seeing, they will let the ghost of a dogma, which rivers of blood have been shed to lay, frighten them from adopting the course which lies before us, broad and plain as the king's highway: The remedy for darkness is light; for ignorance, knowledge; for wrong, righteousness. "

"True enough as an abstraction, my friend; but how shall it be reduced to practice?" queried his listener.

"The Nation nourished and protected slavery.

153

The fruitage of slavery has been the ignorant freed-man, the ignorant poor-white man, and the arrogant master. The impotence of the freedman, the ignorance of the poor-white, the arrogance of the late master, are all the result of national power exercised in restraint of free thought, free labor, and free speech. Now, let the Nation undo the evil it has permitted and encouraged. Let it educate those whom it made ignorant, and protect those whom it made weak. It is not a matter of favor to the black, but of safety to the Nation. Make the spelling-book the scepter of national power. Let the Nation educate the colored man and the poor-white man because the Nation held them in bondage, and is responsible for their education; educate the voter because the Nation can not afford that he should be ignorant. Do not try to shuffle off the responsibility, nor cloak the danger. Honest ignorance in the masses is more to be dreaded than malevolent intelligence in the few. It furnished the rank and file of rebellion and the prejudice-blinded multitudes who made the Policy of Repression effectual. Poor-Whites, Freedmen, Ku-Klux, and Bulldozers are all alike the harvest of ignorance. The Nation can not afford to grow such a crop. "

"But how, " asked the doctor, "shall these citizens of the States be educated by the Government without infringement of the rights of the States?"

"Ah, my good old friend!" said Servosse, rising, and placing a hand upon the other's shoulder, "I will

154

leave you, now that you have brought out for me to worship that Juggernaut of American politics by which so many hecatombs have been crushed and mangled. This demon required a million lives before he would permit slavery to be abolished: perhaps as many more would induce him to let the fettered souls be unbound and made free. "

"You are bitter, my son, " said the old man, rising also, and looking into his companion's eyes with a glance of calm reproof. "Do not indulge that spirit. Be patient, and remember that you would have felt just as we of your native North now feel, but for the glare of slumbering revolution in which you have lived. The man who has been in the crater ought not to wonder at his calmness who has only seen the smoke. I have often thought that St. Paul would have been more for-bearing with his Jewish brethren if he had always kept in mind the miracle required for his own conversion. "

"Perhaps you are right, Doctor, " said the Fool; "but ought not something also be allowed to the zeal of the poor old Jonah who disturbed the slumbers of Nine-veh? At any rate, I leave your question for the Wise Men to answer. I will only say two words about it. The South--that pseudo South which has the power-- does not wish this thing to be done to her people, and will oppose it with might and main. If done at all, it must be done by the North--by the Nation moved, in-stigated, and controlled by the North, I mean--in its own self-defense. It must be an act of sovereignty, an

155

exercise of power. The Nation expected the liberated slave to be an ally of freedom. It was altogether right and proper that it should desire and expect this. But it made the fatal mistake of expecting the freedman to do successful battle on his part of the line, without training or knowledge. This mistake must be remedied. As to the means, I feel sure that when the Nation has smarted enough for its folly, it will find a way to undo the evil, whether the State-Rights Moloch stand in the way, or not."

Appendix 3

A List of Letters and Documents Relating to the Play

A number of unpublished letters relating to the writing and production of the play version of A Fool's Errand were used in the Introduction to this edition. A list of these documents is provided for those who may wish to consult them in more detail. The list is arranged in chronological order.

Twenty-six items are from the Steele MacKaye papers in the Dartmouth College Libraries, Hanover, New Hampshire. They have been designated "Dartmouth" in the list.

Nine letters are from the Albion W. Tourgée papers in the Chautauqua County Historical Society at Westfield, New York. They are designated "AWT Papers" followed by the number assigned to them in the collection.

Two letters were printed in full by Percy MacKaye in his Epoch, The Life of Steele MacKaye... (New York, Boni & Liveright, 1927), volume I, p. 417 and p. 418. They are designated in the list as "Epoch" followed by the page on which they appear.

1	Tourgée to MacKaye	ALS
	7 May 1881	Dartmouth
2	Tourgée to MacKaye	ALS
	20 May 1881	Dartmouth
3	Tourgée to MacKaye	ALS
	7 June 1881	Dartmouth
4	MacKaye to Tourgée	ALS
	8 June 1881	AWT Papers 2406
5	Tourgée to MacKaye	ALS
	10 June 1881	Dartmouth
6	Tourgée to MacKaye	ALS
	14 June 1881	Dartmouth
7	Tourgée to MacKaye	ALS
	21 June 1881	Dartmouth
8	Tourgée to MacKaye	ALS
	5 July 1881	Dartmouth
9	Tourgée to MacKaye	Telegram
	15 July 1881	Dartmouth
10	Tourgée to J.R. Warner	Telegram
	25 July 1881	Dartmouth
11	Tourgée to MacKaye	ALS
	25 July 1881	Dartmouth
12	Howard, H.W.B. to MacKaye	ALS
	25 July 1881	Dartmouth
13	Tourgée to W. Frank O'Brien	Telegram
	26 July 1881	Dartmouth
14	O'Brien, W. Frank to MacKaye	Telegram
	26 July 1881	Dartmouth
15	Tourgée to MacKaye	ALS

	29 July 1881	Dartmouth
16	Tourgée to MacKaye	ALS
	6 August 1881	Dartmouth
17	Tourgée to MacKaye	ALS
	16 August 1881	Dartmouth
18	Tourgée to MacKaye	ALS
	17 August 1881	Dartmouth
19	Tourgée to MacKaye	ALS
	6 September 1881	Dartmouth
20	Tourgée to MacKaye	
	11 September 1881	Epoch, 417
21	Tourgée to MacKaye	ALS
	22 September 1881	Dartmouth
22	Tourgée to MacKaye	ALS
	22 September 1881	Dartmouth
23	Tourgée to MacKaye	
	25 September 1881	Epoch, 418
24	Tourgée to MacKaye	ALS
	27 September 1881	Dartmouth
25	Tourgée to MacKaye	ALS
	10 October 1881	Dartmouth
26	Tourgée to MacKaye	ALS
	15 November 1881	Dartmouth
27	Tourgée, Emma K. to	
	Thomas Dixon, Jr.	TLS draft
	24 February 1906	AWT Papers 9966
28	Dixon, Thomas, Jr. to	
	Emma K. Tourgée	ALS
	4 March 1906	AWT Papers 9982

29	Walker, John B. to	
	Emma K. Tourgée	TLS
	18 March 1906	AWT Papers 10012
30	Tourgée, Emma K. to	
	John B. Walker	TL copy
	20 March 1906	AWT Papers 10017
31	Hulbert, G.S. to	
	Emma K. Tourgée	TLS
	21 March 1906	AWT Papers 10018
32	Walker, John B. to	
	Emma K. Tourgée	TLS
	24 March 1906	AWT Papers 10025
33	Hulbert, G.S. to	
	Emma K. Tourgée	ALS
	28 March 1906	AWT Papers 10028
34	Walker, John B. to	
	Emma K. Tourgée	TLS
	30 March 1906	AWT Papers 10030
35	Tourgée to J.R. Warner	ALS
	no date	Dartmouth
36	Tourgée to J.R. Warner	Telegram
	no date	Dartmouth
37	Contract between Tourgée	
	and MacKaye	draft
	no date	Dartmouth

Appendix 4

Reviews of the Play

The eleven reviews and notices of A Fool's Errand which follow were taken from one of the scrapbooks kept by Albion W. Tourgée and his family and now the property of the Chautauqua County Historical Society at Westfield, New York (item 4330). The first five items are press releases on the play about to be produced. The remaining six items are reviews of the play as produced at the Arch Street Theatre in Philadelphia on October 26, 1881.

THE NORTH AMERICAN /Philadelphia/

"A Fool's Errand" at the Arch.

Messrs. Steele Mackaye and A.W. Tourgee's new play, entitled "A Fool's Errand," will be presented on Wednesday evening, until which time the theatre will remain closed in order to complete arrangements and perfect the rehearsals. The play is a dramatization of Judge Tourgee's well-known novel, of which about one hundred thousand copies have been sold. The author is said to have presented the copyright of his work to his wife, who little dreamed when the novel was first introduced to the public it was destined to net for her especial benefit nearly twenty thousand dollars. The cast of characters includes Mr. Steele Mackaye, Mr. Dominick Murray, Mr. Frank F. Mackaye, Mr. H. Archer and Mr. H. Courtaine. The ladies named are Miss Louise Sylvester, Miss Belle Archer, Miss Helen Mar and others.

Monday October 24, /1881/

LEDGER AND TRANSCRIPT

First Presentation of "A Fool's Errand."

A dramatic event of more than usual note is an-
nounced for Wednesday night of this week at the Arch
Street Theatre. This is the presentation for the first
time of Steele Mackaye's dramatization of Judge Tourgee's "A Fool's Errand." As a rule political novels
are rather more stupid than the run of love stories,
but there are notable exceptions, like "Ten Thousand a
Year," "Uncle Tom's Cabin," and "A Fool's Errand,"
for this last may well rank with the other two, as all
who have read it will understand. As another rule the
dramatization of popular novels is often disappointing,
but this because of lack of capacity in the adapter, for
it is an adapter who more frequently essays the work
than a trained dramatist. "A Fool's Errand" has met
with better fortune through being placed in the hands of
Mr. Steele Mackaye, who understands his art, and who
has devoted much thought and labor to this production.
It has been carefully studied by the members of Mr.
Mackaye's special company containing many finished
actors, has been well rehearsed, and gives promise of

a real success. The first performance, on Wednesday night, is looked forward to with such interest as to cause many persons to make considerable journeys to witness it, and a number of distinguished personages have notified Judge Tourgee of their purpose to be present.

Tuesday, October 25, 1881

"A Fool's Errand."

Elaborate preparations are being made at the Arch-street Theatre for the initial production to-morrow evening of Judge Tourgee and Steele Mackaye's new play, "A Fool's Errand." The author is thoroughly satisfied with the work of Mr. Mackaye, who has brought into the play all the vigor and realism contained in the book itself. All the political element of the story has been eliminated from the dramatization, and the play strengthened by the introduction of new material and fresh characters, making it altogether an interesting story of domestic life in the south. The audience to-morrow evening promises to be a brilliant one, many prominent public men having secured places, and in addition quite a number of New York journalists will grace the theatre on the occasion of the first presentation of what promises to be something entirely out of the usual line of ordinary dramatic work. Judge Tourgee has assisted very much in the work of preparation, and the production will be an event in the history of theatrical affairs in this city.

/October 25, 1881/

THE PRESS [Philadelphia]

A New Play at the Arch

First Production Upon Any Stage of A Fool's Errand

Philadelphia is not often honored with the first hearing of two new plays in a singe [sic] week, but such is the programme for the current week. Lotta brought out on Monday evening the first new piece in which she has acted for more than two years, and this evening, at the Arch-street, A Fool's Errand will have its first performance. The play has been adapted by Steele Mackaye and Judge Tourgee from the novel which made the fame of the latter and lifted him into a notoriety as a novelist as sudden as it was remarkable. Mr. Mackaye has devoted a great deal of time and work to the preparations for the production of the piece and the event will be signalized this evening by the attendance of a large number of prominent personal and political friends of the author, among whom will probably be numbered General Grant and Secretary Windom. The play is called a comedy drama of American life and will be cast as follows: John Burleson, an ex-

Confederate of independent notions, Mr. Steele Mackaye; Colonel Comfort Servosse, an ex-Federal soldier,
One of the Fools, Mr. Herbert Archer; Melville Gurney, a Southern gentleman, who wishes to be let alone,
Mr. Donald Robertson; Jayhu Brown, a Southern Union-
ist, whose life is a mervele, Mr. Harry Courtaine;
Dennis McCarthy, the worst Yankee in the "Wurrld, "
Mr. J. F. O'Brien; Uncle Jerry, a colored "prophet,
priest, and seer, " Mr. F. F. Mackey; Bill Sanders, a
common liver on his own hook, Mr. John Gallagher;
Sam Irvin and Jim Scrogg, "pore whites, " Mr. F.
Desmond and Mr. J. Williams; commander of den No.
12, Tom Morgan; commander of den No. 7, Richard
Gray; Lily Servosse, the Fool's daughter, Mrs. Belle
Archer; Maude Bradley, a nigger school ma'am, Miss
Helen Mar; Achsah, Uncle Jerry's daughter, Miss
Louise Sylvester; Mrs. Metta Servosse, wife of Colonel
Servosse, Mrs. Emma Courtaine; Mary Brown, Maude
Bradley's assistant, Miss Elanore Lane.

                              Wednesday, October 26, 1881

A New American Play.

The first performance of "A Fool's Errand" will take place at the Arch Street Theatre this evening. The drama, as is already known, has been written by Steele Mackaye and A.W. Tourgee from the latter's highly successful novel, and, being distinctly an American play in the fullest sense, will attract more than usual attention. Mr. Mackay plays John Burleson, Herbert Archer Col. Servosse, Harry Courtaine Jayhu Brown and F.F. Mackay Uncle Jerry, while Mrs. Archer takes the part of Lily and Miss Sylvester that of Achsah. This is a good cast, and it will not be the actors' fault if the play be not the success that is hoped for.

October 26, 1881

EVENING TELEGRAPH

Dramatic.

"A Fool's Errand" at the Arch.

A dramatization of Judge Tourgee's novel--we
call it a novel for convenience sake--of A Fool's Errand, by Mr. Steele Mackaye, was represented at the
Arch Street Theatre last night. Mr. Mackaye has
probably done very nearly as much as could be done
towards making a good play from Judge Tourgee's book,
while retaining and giving prominence to the features
upon which Judge Tourgee evidently sets great store.
As the piece stands, it is altogether too talky, too ar-
gumentative, and otherwise too untheatrical for practical stage uses, and it will have to be cut down very
considerably, and if the cuts are judiciously made,
material improvement will be effected. But the play
is not now a strong one, and we do not believe that any
amount of tinkering can make it strong. Judge Tourgee's book has some brilliant writing, and especially
some brilliant descriptive writing, in it, but both in
matter and manner it is essentially undramatic. In
fact, Judge Tourgee's idea in writing it was not the

achievement of dramatic effect at all, but the demonstration of certain of his views and opinions respecting the alleged failure of the reconstruction policy of Congress, and its why and wherefore. Now, the reconstruction policy was a big thing in its way--if we may use such a vulgarism in such a connection--and it gave rise to a good many episodes that might be called dramatic, but it was not dramatic in itself, and the only possible way in which a strong argument for or against it can be made on the stage is by indirection. That is to say, the audience must first be interested in events of a sort that adapt themselves to theatrical representation before they can be expected to become interested in the principles which these events are supposed to be illustrative of. Judge Tourgee, for instance, takes about the same view of the entire wickedness and unquenchable blood-thirstiness of the Southern Ku-Klux that the author--whoever he may be--of the Danites does of the malevolent qualities of the Mormons. It is a master-stroke in The Danites, however, to make the so-called "avenging angels" felt rather than seen. They appear just often enough for the audience to understand distinctly that they are hovering about, and that they are not figments of the imagination, but no effort is made to concentrate the interest on them. Mr. Mackay ⎾sic⏌, in his adaptation of Judge Tourgee's book brings the Ku-Klux to the front, however, and endeavors to let the audience into all their secrets. The result is not edifying, and in some particulars it borders on the

170

ridiculous. Apart from this, however, the play, although it contains a number of incidents that might be made much of, is an extremely weak one. The plot is thin and feebly elaborated, and dramatic coherency seems to have been in some places deliberately violated for the sake of forcing the audience to take cognizance of Judge Tourgee's views. For instance, the assault on "John Bueleson /sic/," by the Ku Kluxes, who mistake him for the Unionist "Colonel Sevosse," is a good enough incident in itself, but it is very weakly executed. And in the next act the raid on "Colonel Sevosse's" house by the friends of "Bueleson /sic/," with the holding of the Worshipful Justice's Court, and the reappearance of "Bueleson /sic/," is full of incidents thas /sic/ so experienced a playwriter as Mr. Mackaye ought to have made much of. This act is very flat, however, and degenerates into broad burlesque just at the very places where it should be theatrically the strongest. The incidents are all good, but the handling of them is to the last degree feeble, while much of the acting is simply ridiculous. A great deal, for instance, might be made of the arming of the negroes and the preparations, with their aid, for a defense. In this act, however, and indeed pretty much all through the play, so far as the negroes are concerned, the minstrel standard is adhered to very uncompromisingly, and with the result of weakening what is already theatrically weak in construction, if not in sentiment. The attempt to represent a gathering of the

171

Ku-Klux in the third act is no more successful than such scenes usually are on the stage--that is to say, it is not successful at all, and the bloodthirsty villains excite risibilities instead of horrors. The conclusion is weak and conventional, and points no moral that we can see, unless it may be that Southern "gentlemen" of Ku-Klux proclivities can only be turned from the errors of their ways by Northern women enticing them to fall in love.

Now, it won't do to say that the fault with this piece is that it treats of an unpleasant subject that is altogether too fresh in the public mind, and concerning which a great diversity of opinions exist. The Octoroon was a success in the old slave-holding days and when party excitement ran very high--a good deal higher than it does now in this part of the world with regard to the Ku-Klux business--but The Octoroon was written from a dramatist's standpoint, and not from the standpoint of a politician. It succeeded because it treated a dramatic subject with a strict regard to practical stage requirements, and with a view to the entertainment of the public rather than for the purpose of advancing the cause of Abolitionism. It would not be easy to make a good play from Judge Tourgee's book without first sinking out of sight its partisanship, and thus effecting an essential reconstruction of some of the incidents which commend the book most positively to the consideration of its readers--or in other words, by eliminating just what its author has the best opinion of.

The best that can be said of the play that has been constructed from <u>A Fool's Errand</u> by Mr. Mackaye is, that it has some fairly good material in it which does not begin to show for what it is worth. The most interesting of the personations last night was the "Jayhu Brown" of Mr. Harry Courtraine. This was a first rate bit of character-acting, and was a first-rate delineation of a representative "poor white." The "Uncle Jerry" of Mr. F. F. Mackay was also a real work of art in its particular line. Miss Louise Sylvester made a "Topsy" out of the character of the negro girl "Achsah, " although the character was conceived on a very different line. The "John Bueleson" /sic7 of Mr. Steele Mackaye was a conventional state "Southron, " but meritorious if we admit the adequacy of the ideal; and the "Bill Sanders" of Mr. John Gallagher was good along similarly conventional lines. Among the ladies the best impression was made by Miss Belle Mackenzie Archer, whose personation of "Lily Servosse" indicates that she has been making rapid advances since she last played here.

/October 27, 1881/

173

Entertainments

Arch Street Theatre--"A Fool's Errand."--It
was only a few minutes before midnight last evening
when the curtain fell, at the Arch Street Theatre, on
the new melo-drama, the joint production of Judge Albion W. Tourgee as author and Steele Mackaye as dramatist, made from the material of Judge Tourgee's
famous book, "A Fool's Errand." Of course it will be
taken for granted that the joint labors of these two gentlemen will have produced something of merit, and the
drama will probably grow in public favor after having
been pruned and trimmed so as to take less than four
hours in its presentation.

The play deals with the troubles in the South
during the reconstruction and "Carpet-bagging" times,
and has a good deal of amusing negro business and
plenty of the thrilling in the Ku-Klux Klan accomplish-
ments. The story as brought out is of a Northern family which has settled in the South. The family consists
of Colonel Servosse, "One of the Fools," his wife and
daughter, Lily, and a white "Nigger Schoolmistress,"

174

Maude Bradley. These characters are taken respec-
tively by Mr. Herbert Archer, Miss Emma Courtaine,
Mrs. Belle Archer (who will be remembered in Philadelphia as Belle Mackenzie, the original Hebe in "Pinafore, ")and Miss Maude Bradley [sic]. Connected with the
fortunes of the family are John Burleson, an ex-Con-
federate of independent notions and a member of the
K. K. K., who has fallen in love with the Yankee school
marm who teaches the "niggers," and who, yielding to
her influence, renounces the Klan, and saves the whole
family from harm. This character is taken by Mr.
Mackaye himself, and he gives a fine impersonation of
a chivalric Southern young gentleman, who, seeing his
errors, has the manliness to acknowledge and abandon
them. Melville Gurney (Mr. Donald Robertson) joins
Burleson in his efforts for the assistance of the Servosse family, for the very good reason that he is se-
cretly married to Lily Servosse and is truly devoted to
her. Mr. F. F. Mackay, so well known here, takes
the part of an old negro of the Uncle Tom order; but
there has probably never been an Uncle Tom so artis-
tically presented in this city as Mr. Mackaye /sic7
does "Uncle Jerry." Miss Louise Sylvester, as Achsah, a colored girl of the Topsy order, also gives an
excellent performance, and Mr. Harry Courtaine is a
very funny Jayhu Brown, a Southern Unionist, "whose
life is a miracle." There are plenty of villains, poor
whites, negroes, &c., in the play; one weird scene of
the meeting of the Ku Klux, the members being dressed

in long black gowns and high pointed caps, with such cheerful emblems as skulls and crossbones, crosses, torches, &c., on them; a plantation scene, where the stage is covered with negroes, and there are some very clever songs and dances, accompanied by guitar, banjo and bones. There are no offensive political features or references in the play. As the author says, and truly, "There is literally no politics in it. Events which also colored politics are used as dramatic incidents to set out a domestic drama of our American life."

The lateness of the hour at which the play closed forbids any attempt to enter into the details of the plot at this time.

/Thursday October 27, 1881/

Dramatic and Musical

"A Fool's Errand"--Its First Production at the Arch.

The fact that nearly the whole of a very large audience remained at the Arch-street Theatre until almost twelve o'clock last night must be assumed as fair evidence that there was more than ordinary attraction in the play which represents in a dramatic form one of the most popular books of the present day. Of Judge Tourgee's book--"A Fool's Errand"--it would be rather superfluous to repeat the favorable criticism which has been confirmed by a sale numbered by hundreds of thousands. For present purpose it need only be said that at the time of its publication there was in the northern mind an anxious desire for familiar acquaintance with the internal condition of the south; and this graphic picture, drawn with a pencil that perhaps insensibly exaggerated some of the defects, was eagerly accepted as accurate, as in the main it has everywhere been acknowledged to be. The book was, however, more than a mere photograph--it was a text book, pointing out, with admirable skill and in a style filled

177

with quaint humor and brilliant aphorisms, the necessities and the difficulties of reconstruction. It would be unfair to assert that such a work, masterly as it is, would in the existing condition of affairs be less warmly received, for the volume itself was no small instrument in so educating the whole country as to have brought about this better state of things; but in its transfer to the stage it must be judged from the standpoint of current events, and not from that of the era which it portrayed. Mr. Mackaye had to grapple in the first place with the problem whether such earnest partisanship as was the motive of the novel could be tempered for mixed audiences, and in the second with the difficulty of concentrating in a few strong situations the interest with which Judge Tourgee had invested so many pages. He deserves the credit of having fairly accomplished both purposes. He has not so tampered with his model as to destroy its identity, and it is rather gratifying for once to see on the stage southern people who are possessed of about the same faults and virtues as the rest of the world and no more, and to witness at the same time the usual northern contrast without the accompaniment of suspenders and catarrh. The story has been a little altered to suit what are called dramatic requirements, and there has been an elaboration of one or two characters for a similar purpose, but as a whole Judge Tourgee would probably acknowledge this as his own child, though Mr. Mackaye has furnished it with a little unaccustomed clothing.

For most plays we believe the performance the first
night serves as a rehearsal to demonstrate where the
alterations shall be made. This should certainly be
so in the present case, for with a desire to give every
one a chance, the playwright has done too much--in
several places whole scenes seem to be without motive,
and much of the business is carried to a surfeit; while
the entire effect of one of the most pathetic of the sit-
uations--when the audience have made up their mind
that the old negro Jerry is dead--is utterly lost by the
absurd anti-climax of bringing the old man again to
life, with no apparent purpose save to speak a "tag"
at the end of the play, for all of the Ku-Klux business
of which he is the centre would be far more effective
over his dead body. There is a great deal in the dialogue that is earnest; but while the words themselves
are properly phrased and sentenced, there is before
the close of the play an appalling sense of surfeit.
This of course Mr. Mackaye can and doubtless will
remedy, as his taste will probably equally suggest the
propriety of cutting out a very large portion of the
"nigger" business. Whether or not this piece will
prove a popular success, after the necessary excisions
have been made, is doubtful; not because of lack of
merit in itself, but because there is scarcely enough
of dramatic action to give it historical interest, and
because to-day the people have nearly forgotten the condition of the south a dozen years ago or less. Social
ostracism still exists, and political supremacy is still

179

possible only to the native white; but the indignities common to the one and the outrages common to the other are no longer apparent in their deformity. If the piece does fail of public support, it certainly will not be for lack of good acting. Mr. Mackaye himself assumed the part of John Burleson and played it with excellent taste, and the other members of the company, especially the ladies, were really admirable. Miss Louise Sylvester, in a Topsy character, Miss Helen Mar, as the young lady from the north teaching the darkey idea how to shoot, and Mrs. Courtaine, as the mother, seemed alike deserving of praise, while by no means least Mrs. Belle Archer, who will be better known to our readers as Miss Belle Mackenzie, "Pinafore's" first Hebe, showed so great an advancement in professional skill, and gave so excellent and easy a performance of Lilly [sic] Servosse, daughter of the northern man who is the hero of the "Fool's Errand, " as to warrant the best hopes for her future. Mr. F. F. Mackay played Uncle Jerry, and as with every character part we have ever seen him assume, the impersonation of the crippled old negro seems to be almost perfect in conception and execution. In the rest of the cast there was nothing notable, except Mr. Harry Courtaine's performance of Jayhu Brown. It was most unlike the author's portrait, but so clever a personation deserves all the greater credit for its originality.

October 27, [1881]

THE PRESS /Philadelphia/

A Fool's Errand

Tourgee and Mackaye's New Play at the Arch-Street.

The real merit of Judge Tourgee's remarkable novel, A Fool's Errand, is sufficiently proved by its enormous popular success, which did far more than appearances on the stump to give the author a national reputation. But the field of the dramatist is much more circumscribed than that of the novelist. The latter may venture into paths forbidden the former, and a publisher may print Nana and L'Assommoir when a manager would not dare to produce either upon the stage. As a political novel Judge Tourgee's work is an important contribution to current literature, but the time is hardly ripe as yet for the dramatic presentation of such a topic. Uncle Tom's Cabin is not yet a favorite play in the South, and Diplomacy and the Danicheffs are not for Russia. Therefore, A Fool's Errand, which was first played last night at the Arch, appeals to only a part of a whole, and its sentiments can never awaken a responsive feeling in the heart of every one in the audience. The polemical character of the

181

work is tempered with a great deal of skill, but the sentiment is always subordinated to it and too evidently accessory rather than essential to the purpose of the play.

The author has set too much store upon his cherished lines to give the dramatist a fair chance. It would be absolutely impossible to deliver the lines set down in the text in less than four hours, and it was dangerously near midnight when the last of the four acts was over, though there had not been a hitch or delay of the slightest nature. Mr. Mackaye will find it necessary to reduce the dialogue in the first act fully one-half and the second nearly as much. When this is done the action will not seem so unimportant in proportion to the dialogue, and the piece will be a good acting play.

Much of the success of last night was due to the acting of the very excellent company which Mr. Mackaye has selected and drilled with painstaking care. A remarkable bit of characterization is the Jayhu Brown of Mr. Harry Courtaine, who has put upon the stage a type of the Southern Corncracker such as Mr. Nast has so often sketched. Striking in appearance and finished in detail, it is an admirable picture. Mr. Mackaye gives considerable individuality to a somewhat conventional character, and Mr. Donald Robertson as Melville Gurney displays a degree of manly earnestness and refined good breeding which are not too often seen on the contemporary stage. Mrs. Belle Archer continues to show steady improvement and increasing force and earnestness. Messrs. Mackay and Gallagher and Miss Louise Sylvester also deserve mention for good acting, and Mr. Maeder set the stage very effectively.

Thursday, October 27, 1881

THE TIMES [London]

"A Fool's Errand."

The First Production of a Political Melodrama
at the Arch Street Theatre.

"A Fool's Errand," a new drama, by Steele
Mackaye and Albion W. Tourgee, was performed for
the first time last evening at the Arch Street Theatre
before a large audience. It is based upon Judge Tourgee's novel of the same name and must be classed as
a political play. A political or polemical play is always open to objection as a work of art, though we
have had some plays of this class, like "Uncle Tom's
Cabin" or "The Octoroon," that being based upon an
everlasting and uncontroverted principle, and having,
besides, a powerful dramatic interest, have attained
popularity and kept it. "A Fool's Errand" is not of
this class. It is a polemical play, but it embodies the
polemics of ten years ago, and illustrates not so much
an enduring principle as an ephemeral phase of political excitement that has passed away and that nobody
cares to recall. The authors of the play, to be sure,

184

have striven hard to make it "non-partisan," but in doing so they have only made more plain the reason why it should not have been written. If it is true, as Colonel Servosse says to Gurney, that the time would come when Southern gentlemen would regret their part in the ku-klux business, and if that time has now come, as we do not doubt, why recall it to them? A Southern audience would not enjoy the reminiscence and it was made very evident last night that a Northern audience does not care for it. Possibly a generation or two hence, when the events referred to have become historical, like the events of "Uncle Tom's Cabin," and we can look back to the period of "reconstruction" without regret and shame and heartburning, a play like this might be listened to, if it were worth it. Just now it is about ten years too late.

The only thing that could have enabled this play to bear down the general objections to a polemical drama was a very strong dramatic action with a very brilliant and forcible dialogue. These conditions, it may as well be said at once, "A Fool's Errand" does not fulfill. The dramatic structure is correct, but commonplace. The action is slow and where strong effects are sought it is in old-fashioned melodramatic situations that have already been worn threadbare. The most of the first act is occupied with an elementary discussion of civil rights, carried on in familiar platitudes by a number of not remarkable characters, who are brought on the stage one by one and make their

185

exits in like deliberate fashion. The audience took
this patiently, occasionally applauding a patriotic period or laughing at a bit of comedy business, and when
the curtain fell upon the stabbing of John Burleson,
which was done in the familiar fashion of the stage.
Mr. Mackaye was rewarded by a complimentary recall.
This was about the last of anything like applause.
Even the negro-minstrel business of the second act
scarcely awakened a response, though there was something like laughter as one after another actor was hand-
ed a letter, strode to the footlights and read it, with
the appropriate expression of horror so familiar to
even the youngest theatre-goers. There had been one
or two letters in the first act; there were no less than
three in the second, and the business became monoto-
nous. When the curtain fell the house was absolutely
silent, and there remained little doubt of the popular
judgment on the play. Nor did the thrilling scene of
the ku-klux in their den, in real ku-klux costumes,
arouse the audience as it was expected to do. Here
was the climax of the play, the "Midnight ride" of
Lily, the shooting of her husband and high tragedy generally; but the audience seemed uncertain whether it
was meant to be funny or not and solved the doubt by
silence.

It ought to be said distinctly that the actors,
with only an occasional lapse and in spite of the pre-
vailing slowness that Mr. Mackaye usually enforces,
did all for the play that was in their power to do. The

186

following is the cast:

John Burleson ----------------- Mr. Steele Mackaye
Colonel Comfort Servosse ------ Mr. Herbert Archer
Melville Gurney --------------- Mr. Donald Robertson
Jayhu Brown ------------------ Mr. Harry Courtaine
Dennis McCarthy -------------- Mr. Frank O'Brien
Uncle Jerry ------------------- Mr. F. F. Mackay
Bill Sanders ------------------ Mr. John Gallagher
Lily Servosse ----------------- Mrs. Belle Archer
Maude Bradley ---------------- Miss Helen Mar
Achsah ----------------------- Miss Louise Sylvester
Mrs. Metta Servosse ---------- Mrs. Emma Courtaine

Mr. Mackaye acts, of course, in his usual deliberate manner, but always intelligently and agreeably, and the other leading parts are sufficiently well played, while one or two "character parts," notably Mr. Courtaine's Jayhu Brown and Mr. Mackay's Uncle Jerry are really admirable. Mr. Courtaine, indeed, made the only conspicuous success of the evening, though Mr. Mackay's Uncle Jerry, a very quiet and dignified study from nature, not from the minstrel stage, is deserving of high praise. Achsah, the old negro's daughter is an eccentric character not in the book; its eccentricity is rather overdone, though it is hard to tell what may have been the author's purpose, the whole treatment of the darkey element being fragmentary and disappointing. It is not worthwhile, however, to criticize the acting in detail. In general it is as good as the play demands or admits, and the failure of "A Fool's Errand" is not

187

due to any fault in its presentation, but to the reason that its dramatic interest is not sufficient to overcome the fatal fault of its ill-chosen motive.

October 27, 1881

PHILADELPHIA AMUSEMENTS

Arch Street Theatre--"A Fool's Errand."

John Burleston /sic/.......... Mr. Steele Mackaye
Colonel Comfort Servosse,
    the "Fool".................. Mr. Herbert Archer
Melville Gurney.............. Mr. Donald Robertson
Jayhu Brown................. Mr. Harry Courtaine
Dennis McCarthy............. Mr. J. F. O'Brien
Uncle Jerry .... Mr. F. F. Mackey
Bill Sanders .... Mr. John Gallagher
Lilly /sic/ Servosse,
    the "Fool's" daughter........ Mrs. Belle Archer
Maude Bradley............... Miss Helen Mar
Achsah .... Miss Louise Sylvester
Mrs. Metta Servosse.......... Mrs. Emma Courtaine

A new play, entitled "A Fool's Errand," written
in collaboration by Judge A.W. Tourgee and Steele
Mackaye, was produced before a large audience at the
Arch Street Theatre, Philadelphia, last night.   It
moved smoothly for a first performance, although it
was well known that very inadequate rehearsal had been
given the play.   As a whole the popular verdict was un-

doubtedly one of warm approval, and, with some changes which Mr. Mackaye will have to make, the play will become a very popular one. The motive is a strong one and clearly defined. The incidents are numberless, while the scenes through which Burleston ⌐sic⌐ passes would seem to have been sufficient to have changed the stony heart of a graven image. The result is surely attained. The process of developing his mental calibre from a bigoted sectionalist to a nationalist occasioned a great deal more trouble to other people than the object was really worth. The love element is almost clever enough to justify all the elaboration which it gets. Absolute disappointment met the so-called Ku-Klux-Klan realism, which was, in plain words, a dead failure. The third act recalls a monstrosity entitled "The Illuminati, " which Mr. Bangs last year induced the innocent Colonel Goodwin to bring out at the Walnut, and which the audience guyed throughout its doleful length the first night and nobody went to see thereafter. For five minutes last evening "A Fool's Errand" was in terrible danger of merciless guying and inevitable collapse. Nothing but the commanding power of declamation which Mr. Mackaye possesses and used at the critical moment saved the third act. We know very well that this Ku-Klux business is one of Judge Tourgee's pet ideas, but he should defer to Mr. Mackaye's more extensive dramatic experience and have the meetings of the Klan take place off the stage.

It may be well to point out the material uses

made of the book and to indicate at the same time the
new characters introduced:--John Burleston *[sic]*, the
bluff Ku Klux of the book, is developed into the leading
character in the drama. Melville Gurney and Lilly
[sic] Servosse (of the midnight ride, chap. 36) are
preserved in their former relations, except that the
love passage between them is assumed to have ante-
dated the opening of the play--a secret marriage having indeed taken place. Maude Bradley, a young Yankee "nigger school ma'am," is a new character. A
friend of Lilly's *[sic]* and inmate of the household at
Warrington, she is obviously introduced in order that
the incidents of her courtship of John Burlston *[sic]*
may constitute the romantic element as contrasted with
the troubles that afflict the married lovers (Lilly *[sic]*
and Melville). Jayhu Brown the quaint old Union man,
with his cough that had done service as an exemption
paper, is preserved bodily and given an important
share of the humorous element of the play. Uncle Jerry, "the prophet, priest and seer" of the colored people, is retained with the same clairvoyant characteristics which he had in the book. Achsah, the daughter
of Uncle Jerry, is a new character (introduced appar-
ently to create a character part for Miss Louise Sylvester *[sic]*), reminding one of a cross between "Top-
sey" and "Meg Merrilles." The intense nervous organization, akin to the solemn religious temperament
of her father, united to an irrestible inclination to mischief, give her weird voudoo proclivities, which are

united with a childlike simplicity and an absolute lack
of knowledge of the world. The Southern negro witch
is an absolutely new character to the stage, and is
capable of great elaboration. Dennis McCarthy, the
Irishman, is the only character absolutely foreign to
the elements of the book. He is introduced as a foil
by his characteristic blunderings united with "his
mother wit, " to the grotesque negro character.
Through his native superstitions he is made for a time
the victim of Achsah's voudooism, with quite comical
results. Bill Sanders is a realistic representative of
the aoler $\sqrt{?}$ but more malicious class of what are
called "the poor whites. " He has been made much
more prominent in the play than in the book. The Ku-
Klux are introduced in costumes copied from veritable
samples of their disguises. The model from which
they were made was captured on the person of a man
taken in the great raid. The Ku-Klux-Klan is used as
the tragic element of the play--the chief situations
arising out of the fact that Burlston $\sqrt{sic}$ and Gurney,
who are in love with the Northern girls, are leaders
of the Klan. The negro element is, as was necessary,
very prominent, but is subordinated to the domestic
tragedy which is constantly threatening but never oc-
curs. Colonel Servosse and his wife are accessories
to the main idea. He is "the Fool" of the book and
the father of Lilly $\sqrt{sic}$, and the type of the Northern
man who dared to go South in defiance of the mandate
of the Klan. In some noticeable instances the dialogue

192

from the book might have been used by the playwrights with absolute certainty of being better than the new words employed to paraphrase the Judge's terse English. With the exception of the pretty School Ma'am the characters invented out of hand do not greatly strengthen the play.

When at a late hour the curtain fell for the last time a great many had gone home, but those who were present called all the favorites to the front of the stage. As the impersonator of the leading character of the play, Mr. Mackaye set himself a task of considerable difficulty. His calmness and his early dramatic education certainly stood him instead last night in critical moments. He was judicious and careful as ever and displayed none of his familiar mannerisms. He was of great and vital service to the play. Mr. F. F. Mackey did not make nearly so striking a character of Uncle Jerry as was expected and the acting of Miss Sylvester as his daughter was at times much overdone. The audience took kindly to the negro songs and dances, especially the weird refrain in the first act, but it did not appear to understand what the authors intended by Achsah's wild mummery. The introduction of the professional tambourine and bones was another phase of that dangerous experiment which the authors call the "third act," and even the gallery tired of endless repetitions that were not called for. Miss Sylvester is a conscientious actress and she has evidently worked very hard to develop her ideas of Achsah, but

she has yet to create the part as well as the excuse
for its presence in the play. Mr. Herbert Archer was
capable of all that his part demanded of him. Some
of the best character acting was done by Harry Courtaine as Jayhu Brown. The authors have given him
too many words, however. Donald Robertson and
Frank O'Brien were fair. Mrs. Belle Archer was
pretty and agreeable as the Colonel's daughter, and
Miss Mar effectively did the small amount of talking
and large amount of love making allotted to her.

/October 27, 1881/